Athene Series
Feminist Scholarship on
Culture and Education

(continued)

FEMINIST SCIENCE EDUCATION

Angela Calabrese Barton

ATHENE
SERIES

TEACHERS COLLEGE PRESS
Teachers College, Columbia University
New York and London

Published by Teachers College Press, 1234 Amsterdam Avenue, New York, NY 10027

Library of Congress Cataloging-in-Publication Data

Barton, Angela Calabrese.
    Feminist science education / Angela Calabrese Barton.
        p.   cm. — (Athena series)
    Includes bibliographical references and index.
    ISBN 0-8077-6924-6 (alk. paper). — ISBN 0-8077-6293-8 (pbk. :
alk. paper)
        1. Science—Study and teaching (Higher)—United States.
2. Feminism and education—United States. 3. Barton, Angela
Calabrese. 4. Science teachers—United States—Biography. 5. Women
college teachers—United States—Biography. I. Title. II. Series.
Q183.3.A1B37   1998
507'.1'1073—dc21   97-49819

ISBN 0-8077-6293-8 (paper)
ISBN 0-8077-6294-6 (cloth)

Printed on acid-free paper
Manufactured in the United States of America

05 04 03 02 01 00 99 98   8 7 6 5 4 3 2 1

Contents

Preface

I have often been asked, What is the difference between feminist science teaching and just plain good science teaching? Behind this question is the idea that good science teaching is concerned with teaching science to all students, regardless of race, class, or gender. What is the difference between feminist science teaching and plain good science teaching? is a difficult question to answer because, like those offering the argument with which I am always presented, I, too, believe that feminist science teaching, like nonfeminist science teaching, when carried out with a great deal of thoughtfulness, planning, and reflection, is good teaching. Any teaching that seeks to actively involve the learner and her or his experiences in the mediated construction of knowledge in meaningful, relevant, inclusive, and nurturing ways is good teaching.

Yet feminist science teaching is concerned with much more than creating inclusive pedagogical strategies to help all students become literate in the content and process of Western science. It is political and activist and deeply concerned with questions that emerge from the intersections of the pedagogical, the disciplinary, and the personal and with the political, social, and historical dimensions of each of these. It is also concerned with how knowledge of the ways in which these domains intersect with teachers and students in science classrooms is functional *and* productive. Feminist teaching constantly questions how relationships and knowledge are situated within discourses of knowledge and power, the impact this has on the teacher and the learner, and how it is that the teacher and the learner can utilize this embeddedness of science and self to understand and transform the individual, society, and science.

Thus, in addition to helping all students learn science, feminist science teaching attempts to expose the cultural, social, and historical dimensions of the culture and practice of science—as it is situated within the classroom and within the larger society—in order to help students understand and act upon the ways in which science and the self-in-science have been constructed historically. Further, through situating

science and the self within the larger discourses of power and knowledge, feminist science teaching utilizes the themes of individual and
collective agency so that creating new ideas about and relationships in
science become possibilities.

This perspective that views feminist science teaching as more than
just good science teaching is best described by adherents of Women in
Science Education [WISE], a study group that has helped me find the
space in which to explore feminist science teaching and researching over
the past 6 years. Members of Women in Science Education [WISE] (1996)
argue that science teaching must be both political and activist because of
the teacher's critical position and participation in the process of teaching
and because of the explicit desire to create a more just world through
teaching. Feminist science education challenges the ideologies that justify power inequalities and utilizes that knowledge to break silences,
disrupt power relations, articulate what is possible, construct different
realities, and experiment with alternative ways of learning and knowing. In this sense, feminist science education embraces a liberating sense
of science: Understanding is aided by a recognition of science as a human construction, both permeated and bounded by rules and expectations that have grown out of and continue from social and political
identities, beliefs, and interests (WISE, 1995).

In its liberatory, political, and activist intentions, feminist theory
provides an innovative lens with which to reflect on inclusiveness in
science education. The conceptual framework central to this effort stems
from attempts to rethink the nature of science and science education
rather than from a belief that equality in the sciences can be reached
through the implementation of compensatory programs for women and
minorities. This marks a fundamental shift in thinking in science education circles: it shifts the reform focus from deficiencies held by women
or minorities to deficiencies and discriminatory practices in science and
education. This shift in thinking raises such questions as, Can a science
and science education be constructed that is liberatory rather than oppressive for those students who historically have been marginalized by
the science endeavor? and, Can we teach a science that is open to multiple ways of knowing in order to help *all* students value the contributions
made by those traditionally silenced in science?

In the teaching and researching that I do and that I write about in
the chapters to follow, I utilize this shift in thinking to argue that feminist theory pushes against the boundaries of the conversation regarding
teaching science to all students through the construct of ''liberatory
education.'' As a teacher and researcher, I have found this construct
helpful, for it has sighted the need to uncover power relations embed-

ded within, and controlling of, the discourses and practices in education and in science (Freire, 1970; Gore, 1993; Harding, 1986, 1991; Weiler, 1988). Liberatory education in science is based on the recognition that teachers and students are agents and actors who actively and collectively shape and reshape their own understandings of the world and themselves from historically and culturally determined standpoints. These standpoints are manifestations of multiple and conflicting contexts, each of which imposes other relationships of power, privilege, values, and role definitions both inside and outside of science.

Thus, as a feminist science educator interested in liberatory science education, I feel that it is necessary to understand science teaching and learning in their contexts. It is necessary to understand the ways in which my explorations, analyses, or attempts to create "science for all" in my classroom are embedded in my own situational understandings of science, knowledge, and power, and how they are also embedded in my own and my students' histories and identities. I believe that the positional nature of science teaching and learning must be explored in order to develop deep and contextual understandings of what it means to teach science for all. Reflexively, it is also important to understand how a teacher's understanding of the positional nature of teaching and learning can open up possibilities for a more liberatory education in science for all students. These two intertwined issues, deeply rooted in the feminist attempt to understand the situatedness of gender relations and knowledge within the larger context of disciplinary power, guide the teaching, researching, and writings in this book. In what follows, I develop the idea of positionality and its potential role in feminist liberatory science teaching and learning and in teacher research. I also use my situated role as a teacher-researcher who is developing understandings of the positional nature of teaching and learning to explore possibilities for a more liberatory education in science for all students.

Acknowledgments

I am grateful to the students in my introductory chemistry classes, who courageously stood up both to science and to me. I have learned much from the complexity and contradictions in their lives, which they sometimes refused to give up to learn chemistry.

I would like to thank Kathleen Roth for being so generous in sharing herself—her insight, ideas, teaching, time, and friendship. I thank her for helping me find a space in which to think and write about feminist theory and science teaching. I am grateful to Lynn Paine, Wanda May, and Gail Richmond for their insight, support, and encouragement. I give sincere thanks to Sandra Hollingsworth for helping me believe in the importance of my personal experience and ways of knowing.

To my very good friends in the Women in Science Education group at Michigan State University, Kathy, Constanza, Elaine, Lori, Margery, Lynne, Deb, and Gail: my thanks for providing me a safe place in which to explore feminist issues in science. My thanks to Peggy for her insight, support, and friendship. I would also like to thank Brian Ellerbeck at Teachers College Press for his support and practical advice at various stages of this book.

A special thank you to the faculty at Ashton Community College for allowing me to teach there and to study my teaching.

My thanks to my family—my parents, Ray and Barb Calabrese, and my sisters, Prudence, Cathy, Michelle, and Christine—who gave me hours of comic relief over the phone and by mail and E-mail. A special note of gratitude to my parents, whose words and actions have sparked my own interest in social justice and liberatory education.

Finally, my thanks to my best pal, Scott. I thank him for giving me the space I needed in which to be a teacher-researcher, for his intellectual and spiritual companionship, and for bringing the complexity and contradictions in his life to reading and critiquing my work.

Feminist Liberatory Science Education?

Prejudice has also been present in the development of science, but not many people know about what minorities go through to have their theories accepted. I feel that science, like any other area of society, needs a lot of revision. People should not be ignored because of their culture. All people are capable of being an asset to the science community and should be allowed to do so, especially in science class. (Julianna, journal entry, April 1994)

TEACHER: What scares you the most in science class?
TRACY (student): My ideas being way out there or I guess the white male structure, the discrimination. . . . One thing is very evident, at least in the book that we used: very rarely is a woman's name mentioned, and I think that I have become more aware of this. Women are practically nonexistent. You know that is not the way that [it] happened. I don't like this kind of elitism in anything. That is the idealist in me and I like the idea of making it more real to everyone. Whatever level they are at, whatever age they are, whatever race, whatever, money, whatever, so that people can understand it or at least have the opportunity to understand it their own way without fearing that they are going to be excluded. (Conversation, June 15, 1994)

Tracy and Julianna were two students from an introductory "bridging" chemistry course that I taught at an urban community college in the midwestern United States. Both were older than the traditional college student. Both attended the community college part-time in the evening, working during the day as a secretary and waitress, respectively. Both had little formal education beyond high school. Tracy and Julianna were enrolled at the community college because it offered a diverse and flexible evening program, small classes, and manageable tuition. The financial issue is important because many of my students at the college held low-paying jobs, were single mothers, or had other financial constraints that took precedence over formal education.

Despite their lack of formal higher education, both Tracy and Julianna expressed insight into what it means to teach and learn science across race, class, and gender. They spoke openly about their dislike for science and, in particular, the ways in which the science that they were required to learn at school had little to do with who they were as people. Tracy's fear about "being excluded" by her desire to understand science her own way and Julianna's experience of being ignored as a result of her Mexican heritage highlight only too well messages that had infiltrated their education in science—that their gender, race, or class or a combination of these is implicitly inferior and unwelcome in the neighborhood of science.

FIRST WAVE FEMINISM IN SCIENCE EDUCATION: ISSUES OF EQUITY

Equity Issues

Tracy's and Julianna's experiences of being discriminated against and silenced in science class follow a 30-year period marked by advances toward equity in the policies and practices guiding the education of women and minorities in science. The outcomes of studies of equity coupled with the lagging scores of U.S. students on international science exams have led the science education community to concentrate their efforts on constructing and promoting conceptual understandings and scientific literacy for all students in science (American Association for the Advancement of Science [AAAS], 1989). Since this reemergence of "science for all" as a national goal in the United States in the 1980s, research studies and theoretical debates have been conducted to make sense of the ways in which efforts toward scientific literacy for all have been inclusive and supportive of the needs of those groups of children who have historically been marginalized by school science (Atwater, 1996; Barton, 1997b; Barton & Osborne, 1995; Brickhouse, 1994; Cobern, 1996; Eisenhart, Finkel, & Marion, 1996; Kahle & Meece, 1994; Roychoudhury, Tippins, & Nichols, 1993, 1995; Stanley & Brickhouse, 1995; WISE, 1994, 1995).

Clearly, questions of science for all have been linked, in part, to debates about equity in science education. The reemergence of the women's movement in the 1960s, along with the civil rights movement, led the science education community to take a hard look at the kinds of opportunities being granted to girls and minorities. This wave of critiques of practices and their resulting reforms, referred to in women's studies as "first wave feminism" or "liberal feminism" focused on the inferior treatment received by girls and minorities in schools and in other informal science education programs. The liberal feminist perspective played an extremely important role in the development of science education programs because it shifted the emphasis from the ways in which girls and minorities were "inferior" and placed it on the kinds of structural and institutional constraints that posed barriers to successful participation in science by girls and minorities (Brickhouse, 1994).

Impact of First Wave Feminism on Science Education

The impact of liberal feminism on science education cannot be understated. It has influenced science education programs in profound ways. First, liberal feminist studies have emphasized ways of bringing women and minorities "into science" by focusing on achievement, attitudes, and participation in science (Kahle & Meece, 1994; Mullis & Jenkins, 1988; Young & Fraser, 1994). For example, these studies have been helpful in pointing out the myriad ways in which women and minorities have been both actively and passively blocked from entering the sciences in numbers equal to those of their white male counterparts: classroom activities that promote perceptions of science as dull, only for smart people, only for boys, and not connected with personal experience; a lack of role models, after-school programs and incentives; science teaching practices that perpetuate scientific knowledge as objective, rational, male, and mechanistic; family and home structures that promote traditional roles for women; and educational practices that emphasize boys' over girls' achievements in science (Kahle & Meece, 1994). In short, these studies have pinpointed a series of external factors that have made equal opportunity in science unequal across race, class, and gender.

The liberal feminist perspective has, moreover, played a role in creating programs and opportunities to get more girls into science and to help them achieve there. These programs and opportunities include demasculinizing and demystifying science by exposing girls to role models and career information, improving girls' self-confidence as well as their perceptions of their ability to do science, implementing teaching strategies that actively involved girls in science lessons, developing girls' skills in science, offering experience with a variety of science activities, including field trips, and providing laboratory exercises (Kahle & Meece, 1994). However, in this phase, science itself, as a practice or a culture, was not critiqued or made problematic within the science or science education community.

SECOND WAVE FEMINISM IN SCIENCE EDUCATION: GENDER-INCLUSIVE SCIENCE

As the feminist presence in science education grew, so also did the sophistication of its critique. The first wave, liberal feminism, was followed by a second wave that began to impact science education in the 1980s and 1990s. One of the most significant results to emerge from second wave feminist studies in science education has been the challenge to the values and standards of science and science education. Such studies have moved beyond liberal efforts at equity, which tackled the problems of girls and minorities in science by placing the onus of responsibility for change on those who are already marginalized. Many of these new feminist studies have highlighted a need to explore multiple ways of knowing and doing science that are reflective of the social, historical, and political context in which science has been constructed and in which students learn that science (Barton, 1995; Barton & Osborne, 1995; Brickhouse, 1994; Roychoudhury, Tippins, & Nichols, 1993, 1995; WISE, 1994, 1995). Second wave feminist studies in science education have focused on "the nature and practice of science" and on "ways of knowing in science." The arguments are premised on the belief that science is not a practice completely separated from other ways of knowing and doing. It is connected to, and influenced by, ways of knowing and doing that permeate every other aspect of life, from religion to survival, and that the knowledge produced within the science community is not value-free or independent.

Feminist Analyses of Science

In this phase, feminist research in science education began to draw heavily on the work of feminist philosophers of science, such as Sandra Harding (1986) and Evelyn Fox Keller (1985), and in particular on their analysis of the positivistic tradition of science. Because of the large influence that second wave feminist critiques have had on feminist work in science education, it is worth describing in some detail the nature of these critiques.

Since the birth of positivistic science in the 17th century, positivism has developed into one of the most powerful intellectual traditions in contemporary Western society. It has dominated the thought, culture, and practices of science, as well as of many other disciplines (Carr & Kemmis, 1989; Toulmin, 1990). Since the 17th century, scientific ideology—its values, goals, and assumptions (Fox Keller, 1985)—has expanded, but its essential nature has been maintained. The major premise that has served and continues to serve as the foundation for modern science posits that all scientific facts are grounded in sound scientific theory, largely free of personal, social, and cultural values and distorted one-way views of the world (Harding, 1991; Longino, 1990). This positivistic ideology is reflected in the scientific premise of objectivity, in the reductionist presentation of the nature of science and scientific knowledge, and in the authoritarian nature and powerful position of science in society.

Nature of Science and Scientific Knowledge. Feminist scholars (Bleier, 1986; Harding, 1986, 1989, 1991; Hubbard, 1990; Longino, 1989, 1990) question the positivist notion of objectivity and the value and gender neutrality of scientific knowledge. They ask a question that is based solidly in a social constructivist epistemological framework: Does value-free science exist? The answer is no—at least not in this society—for several reasons. As Longino (1990) suggests, there are two types of values relevant to science: constitutive values—those that determine acceptable scientific practices or methods, and contextual values—those personal, social, and cultural values that involve the societal process in which science is done. Whereas proponents of the concept of value-free modern science suggest that these two types of values are disparate, feminist scholars believe that contextual values are intimately linked to the constitutive and thus play a role in scientific inquiry.

For example, scientific inquiry is never completely spontaneous; it always has a guide, whether it be curiosity, circumstance, or achievement. It is consequently vulnerable to human action and interaction. According to the feminist argument, to recognize the inaccuracy of a value-free labeling in science, one only has to see how subservient is scientific inquiry to social and cultural interests. A visit to the library or the bookstore would generate a lengthy list of science books written specifically with cultural and social interests in mind (Longino, 1989). Furthermore, scientific questions often emerge from certain political, cultural, and socioeconomic frameworks, and data are interpreted synonymously. Society thus acts as a leader, guiding scientific inquiry and conclusion making down its own self-serving path (Hubbard, 1990). Finally, commitment to a particular scientific model is controlled by such frameworks, which more often than not are based solely on power and possession (Longino, 1989). Researchers are dependent on outside sources for funding and recognition. They ask and often answer questions in light of that dependency. Admission of these influences disallows the assumption of value-free science.

Feminist scholars further argue that scientific knowledge, because of its vulnerability to human action and interaction, is also highly predisposed to personal bias. Harding (1991) maintains that because the present discipline has been shaped exclusively by men, science is male oriented or male biased and that at present the discipline is imbued with European, middle-upper-class, and heterosexual values. It therefore presents a partial or distorted view of the world and represents an excluding knowledge. In evolutionary studies, for example, a great deal of attention has been placed on interactional behavior in its relation to the development of human anatomy (Harding, 1986; Hubbard, 1990; Longino, 1989, 1990). This has been studied in great detail and used as a potential argument for biologically determined sex roles (Harding, 1986). The studies, according to Harding, "show a high tendency to project onto ape nature and social relations both racist and sexist projects of the observer's own society" (p. 96) and have been used to justify and perpetuate masculine dominance and restriction of women's opportunities (p. 83). Harding asserts that "androcentric assumptions . . . appear in the collection, interpretation, and use of the data" (p. 96) and that this is a blatant example of value-filled science and that there are many more subtle ones that probably never get picked up on because of the value system deeply embedded in our daily lives.

In pursuit of the elimination of androcentric science, Harding (1986, 1991) contends that the recognition of gender, and the individual, structural, and symbolic consequences of it that account for woman's oppression, provides a lens through which scientists can and must view the world. A woman's experience is equally as valid a resource as a man's: Scientific inquiry must allow questions that originate in women's experiences. Furthermore, women's perspectives on their own experiences provide "important empirical and theoretical resources for research. . . . They generate research problems and the hypotheses and problems that guide research. They also serve as a resource for the designing of research projects, the collection and interpretation of data, and the construction of evidence" (1989, p. 28). Until gender is recognized, science will remain gender exclusive.

Feminist scholars thus agree that value-free, gender-free science does not, and probably in our society cannot, exist. For it to exist, the construction of scientific knowledge would have to eliminate bias (Longino, 1989), not by trying to control all external and internal influences that act upon its social construction, but, rather, by a reflexive understanding and acknowledgment of their influence. Such a scientific prospect as gender-free science, because of its highly interactive, complex, and subjective nature, would embrace many female values, in addition to, but not to the exclusion of, many already influential male values (Longino, 1989). If science is ever to become value or gender free, scientists must recognize and acknowledge the social forces that shape their beliefs (Harding, 1991; Longino, 1989). They must also listen to and theorize from the standpoint of all marginalized groups in order to recognize otherwise hidden biases (Harding, 1991). This will enable the constructor of knowledge to create scientific statements that are more inclusive through a more complete understanding of the social forces that shape knowledge.

Ways of Knowing. Scientific ways of knowing science is a second area analyzed by second wave feminists. The idea that scientists learn by distancing themselves from their object of study, that they can control their environment and their object, and that they must separate and fragment knowledge so that it can be classified and categorized has been problematized. Ruth Hubbard (1986) captures the spirit of this separation and fragmentation of science: "Scientists attain their objectivity by looking upon natural phenomena (including other people) as isolated objects that exist outside the context of interrelationships in which human beings are a part. Scientists describe their observations as though they and their activities existed in a vacuum" (p. 20).

Feminist scientists and philosophers question why one method of systematically interacting with nature and using knowledge gained from that interaction may be categorized as acceptable whereas other methods are not. As Martin (1988) suggests, perhaps it is because the "uniqueness and complexity of individuals are viewed as problems to be overcome by science, not as irreducible aspects of nature; personal feelings and relationships are taken to be impediments of objectivity, not ingredients of discovery" (p. 130). Indeed, feminist scholars agree that personal feelings and relationships are ingredients of discovery because of the complexity of individuals and their intricate relationships to the world. As Hubbard (1986) notes, scientists must recognize both context and subjectivity as parts of science, because they are part of being human.

Hence, feminist scientists argue that science and its way of knowing and relating to the world must be viewed in more complex and holistic terms. Traditional science, furthermore, by suggesting that there exists only one correct method of obtaining those little segments of science, simplifies the multitude of ways of relating to and understanding the world. Finally, by trying to categorize all the small pieces of the world so that it is understandable by others, they separate it, and in doing so contribute to distortions of reality. Science thus becomes a "disembodied application of a set of rules" (Longino, 1990, p. 13).

Such feminist analyses of ways of knowing in science have been supported by feminist studies in psychology and "women's ways of knowing" (Belenky, Clinchy, Goldberger, & Tarule, 1986; Gilligan, 1982). These studies have highlighted how girls are socialized to view the world holistically. Girls are taught to value relationships, connections, and caring. Feminist psychologists show how these ways of knowing have been devalued in masculinized society. Moral development, for example, has been theorized through male worldviews (Gilligan, 1982). More important to feminist studies in science education, according to this perspective, is the fact that the scientific worldview has also been developed around male ways of knowing. This has led to an emphasis on reason, logic, mechanism, and reductionism over the more female ways of knowing.

Relationship Between Science and Society. A third area in which feminists have analyzed science is in its relationships with society. Scientists' aim, since the 17th century, has been the control and the domination of nature (Fox Keller, 1985). Francis Bacon once wrote that science should lead to the sovereignty, dominion, and mastery of "man" over nature, the "command of nature in action" (quoted in Fox Keller, 1985, p. 34); through the powerful objective reasoning characteristic of science, human beings can control the world. Bacon's writings display the very essence of the strength and power of traditional science. Science is recognized in our society as invincible because it claims to have "finally found the correct method for achieving results" (Feyerabend, 1988, p. 37). Scientific facts are consequently treated in schools with the same respect with which religious facts were treated only a century ago. The judgment of the scientist is received with the same reverence with which those of bishops and cardinals were received not too long ago (p. 37). Fox Keller (1985) equates this power picture with paranoia:

> Grounded in the fear of being controlled by others rather than in apprehension about the loss of self-control, in the fear of giving in to others rather than to one's own unwelcoming impulses, the attention of paranoid is rigid, but it is not narrowly focused. Rather than ignore what does not fit, he or she must be alert to every possible clue. . . . Everything must fit. . . .

All clues fit into a single interpretation . . . with no room for alternative explanations. (p. 121)

Fox Keller goes on to suggest that this need to have only one interpretation is the need to measure one's own strength against another's submission; it is the dream of the dominion of science over nature (p. 124). Feminist scholars, as does Fox Keller, suggest that science is not an exercise of domination, but, rather, one of equity. As Fox Keller notes, one contemporary cancer scientist believes that "if you really want to understand a tumor, you've got to be a tumor" (p. 125).

In addition to being part of the societal power pyramid, traditional science has its own, internal, power pyramid based on competition, capital, and control. Longino (1989) suggests that science labs are typically structured hierarchically and that scientists relate to one another through competition. These two features of traditional science—the hierarchical organization of scientific knowledge and of scientists within society and within the discipline, and competition—are not necessarily a feature of science, but, rather, simply androcentric features of Western society to which Western society has grown accustomed (Harding, 1986).

In short, second wave feminists suggest that the discipline of science demands that the perspectives and insights of women, minorities, and working-class students who have been kept from participating in the inner circle of science be included (Harding, 1991). Incorporating the lived experiences of all people, but especially the experiences of the groups still struggling for a space in science, makes possible the construction of an inclusive science and science education. Fox Keller (1985) describes this need:

> A healthy science is one that allows for the productive survival of diverse conceptions of mind and nature, and of correspondingly diverse strategies. In my vision of science, it is not taming nature that is sought but the taming of hegemony. To know the history of science is to recognize the mortality of any claim to universal truth. Every past vision of scientific truth, every model of natural phenomena, has proved in time to be more limited than its adherents claimed. The survival of productive difference in science requires that we put all claims for intellectual hegemony in their proper place—that we understand that such claims are, by their very nature, political rather than scientific. (pp. 178–179)

These feminist analyses of science from a social constructivist standpoint represent a significant shift in thinking in science education because they refute the positivist myth that there is an objective, solitary way of doing science that results in independent, unbiased knowledge. The positivistic myth is shown to be false when science is seen to be a human endeavor and therefore subject to human biases, social conditions, and ambitions (Fox Keller, 1985; Harding, 1987, 1991; Longino, 1990). These biases infiltrate every part of science, including its norms, beliefs, values, discursive practices, and ways of acting and reasoning.

Impact of Second Wave Feminism on Science Education

This summary of feminist analyses of science points toward the focus and scope of second wave feminism in science education. Like feminist analyses of the sciences, second wave feminist science education research has been grounded in a social constructivist framework (Roychoudhury, Tippins, & Nichols, 1995). As a result of these studies in the history and philosophy of science and psychology, questions around the social construction of such female-friendly and gender-inclusive science have begun to emerge. Feminist researchers in science education have used the movement to understand science as a social construct to spark debate about ways of knowing science and the implications that this has for science for all (Barton & Osborne, 1995; Eisenhart, Finkel, & Marion, 1996).

Incorporating Marginalized Ways of Knowing. Building on the idea that children need to understand the social aspect of science and the connection that this has to the nature of science and scientific knowledge construction, some feminist researchers have argued that science teachers utilize the social element in science to value ways of knowing, doing, and acting that traditionally have not been part of the practice of science. Brickhouse (1994) argues that narrowly defined scientific ways of knowing, such as rational thinking that has been separated from feeling and emotion and ideas separated from context and personal experience are particularly problematic for female students, because many women value knowledge that is relational, oriented more toward sustaining connection than toward achieving autonomy. This woman-centered perspective is in opposition to school knowledge, which is often characterized by reason and abstract rules, mastery over nature, and authority over others (Luttrell, 1993). Such a vision of science is often dull and abstracted and results in a high level of female student alienation from science. Feminist science educators thus argue that one role of science teachers ought to be to utilize students' experiences outside of science (e.g., traditionally female activities and interests such as prenatal testing, child care, and cooking) to create a more inclusive science (Howes,

1997; Osborne, 1995; WISE, 1995). It has also been argued that certain "women's ways of knowing" such as caring, cooperation, and compassion ought to be used to help teachers and students define and defend scientific understandings (Roychoudhury, Tippins, & Nichols, 1993, 1995).

Gender-Inclusive Science. The conceptual framework central to these efforts focuses on rethinking the nature of science and science education rather than on trying to reach equality in the sciences through the implementation of compensatory programs. This shift has propelled efforts at equity toward a search for the ways in which the traditional discursive practices and epistemological and ontological assumptions of Western science can be marginalizing to large groups of students (Atwater, 1996; Roychoudhury, Tippins and Nichols, 1993, 1995). One direct outgrowth of this research has been the development of a gender-inclusive science education (Roychoudhury, Tippins, & Nichols, 1995). This has involved two areas: what type of science gets taught and how it is taught. A gender-inclusive science in the classroom is based on a social constructivist perspective and can be defined through four general characteristics. First, scientific knowledge is acknowledged as culturally and socially bound. Embedded within the gender-inclusive science curriculum is a study of the social context that has influenced the study of particular areas of science, and the effect of this context on the scientific ideas developed and accepted within the scientific community. Second, scientific knowledge is reflective of nature's holistic, interactive, and complex existence. Scientific models used in the classroom would "stress context rather than isolated traits and behaviors, interactive rather than linear relations, democratic rather than authoritarian models of order in both research and nature" (Harding, 1991, p. 300). Third, the scientific contributions of women and minorities, including those who have not been formally recognized by the community of scientists, are incorporated into a historical analysis of the development of scientific knowledge. For example, the works of Beatrix Potter could be part of a botany course. Fourth, science is practiced through multiple ways of knowing, including, but not limited to, "women's ways of knowing" such as collaboration, cooperation, and caring. Roychoudhury, Tippins, and Nichols (1993, 1995) illustrate this kind of science and science teaching in elementary teacher education through the use of female activities to help preservice teachers develop understandings in classical physics.

Teaching a gender-inclusive science in schools is a daunting task, for it requires a change in the ways that teachers are prepared to teach science. Teachers need to enter the teaching profession with a special knowledge of subject matter and the student body to engage students from diverse backgrounds in meaningful and participatory learning. Teachers need to know more than what is conventionally included in the school curriculum—facts, theories, and procedures fundamental to their subject matter; teachers need to have a thorough understanding of science, including its content, history, culture, and discursive practices, as well as an understanding of student populations and educational processes, so that they can provide opportunities for personally relevant engagement in science by a wide variety of students. Without this extensive knowledge, teachers will lack the ability to construct and implement a compelling repertoire of activities needed to help students conceptually understand the knowledge base of science and to engage in scientific discourse and practice. For these reasons, feminist studies in science education have called for the learning of science to be much more than the learning of facts, theories, and procedures. Learning science also means learning about the norms, beliefs, values, discursive practices, and ways of acting and reasoning that are acceptable within the community of scientists (WISE, 1994, 1995). It also means understanding the ways in which, and the reasons for which, they have been constructed and the implications that this has for those "outside the community of scientists" who wish to enter it or simply communicate with those inside it (Barton & Osborne, 1995; Brickhouse, 1994; Hazelwood, 1996; Roth, 1995). For example, Roth (1995) has illustrated through her work with elementary children that science teachers need to find new kinds of ways of helping their students enter the neighborhood of science (besides helping them master content and process) if that very neighborhood is alienating or dangerous. Barton and Osborne (1995) have argued that to make a science inclusive of "all Americans," the ways of knowing and doing science of those not traditionally part of science culture must be validated and connections and divergences between such experiences and the traditional ways of knowing and doing science must be made explicit.

The move toward a gender-inclusive science is important. It is commonly accepted within the science education community, from both feminist and nonfeminist perspectives, that science in schools is often portrayed as static, objective, rational, and mechanistic. School science promotes this kind of representation through classroom talk and activities, through textbooks, and through which ideas are assessed and how. Roychoudhury, Tippins, and Nichols (1993, 1995), among others, point out that many science classroom activities (even those that are "student centered" and "hands-on") place great emphasis on learning technical jargon and irrefutable facts, separated from conceptual understandings and decontextualized from their social, historical, cultural, and political contexts. Edwards and Mercer (1987) help us to see through classroom dialogue that the teacher's position of authority can be used to selectively emphasize, interpret, and reconstruct students' comments. This enables the teacher to guide the discourse toward the "correct," predetermined answers at which the students must arrive. Because the correct answers developed from the positivist tradition, the teacher can often choose to highlight the more "rational" and "intellectual" over emotional, personal, and other "nonscientific" ideas. This scientific pedagogical discourse induces students "to think and make judgments according to the constraining influences of a [positivistic] paradigm and to this extent, pedagogy selectively excludes alternatives" (Prelli, 1989, pp. 91–92). Thus, students are taught to talk a rigidly defined science. Many studies have highlighted how courses defined by textbooks help students to construct a narrow vision of science—science as a static conglomeration of facts and theories (Anderson, 1991; Kahle & Meece, 1994). Even though students might understand the "in-progress" nature of such facts and theories, they have a difficult time making sense of the conceptual and technological tools and activities that are used to construct those statements. Gender-inclusive science has challenged all of these factors to enact a science education that is reflective of all members of society.

THIRD WAVE FEMINISM IN SCIENCE EDUCATION: SITUATED KNOWING AND LEARNING

Situated Knowing and Learning

The first two waves of feminism in science education have been characterized by a focus on "gender and education" (Luke & Gore, 1992). Analysis tended to expose classroom and curricular inequalities in efforts to equalize imbalanced classroom practice and curricular representation. Throughout these periods, the results of gender and education research led to gender-inclusive curricula and greater access to science for girls. Curricular texts gave girls equal representational space, although not always equal tasks. There was a growing interest in feminist pedagogy that emerged with the growing discontent with patriarchical schooling and utilized gender as an analytic category for understanding discourse and knowledge construction. Both of these waves are characterized by being separatist in nature, utilizing differences between genders as a way of creating inclusiveness and equality.

Yet because first and second wave feminist theory has grown out of women's lived experiences of being oppressed by men and male structures, much of the academic work published by feminists has historically totalized women's experience within social and cultural characteristics shared by many white, bourgeois, intellectual women (hooks, 1981). Claims for women's ways of knowing and for gendered expectations were based on an excluding and essentialistic notion of what it means to be female. As bell hooks (1981) argues in *Ain't I a Woman: Black Women and Feminisms*, this standpoint further marginalized working-class and minority women.

Since the second wave of feminist writing in the 1970s, there has been a slowly growing emphasis on the sociological "trifocal" lens of race, class, and gender as significant dimensions of radical political feminist discourse (Amos & Parmar, 1981; Anyon, 1984; Gaskell, 1992; Luke & Gore, 1992; Middleton, 1993; Weiler, 1988). As Kathleen Weiler (1988) writes, "The ways in which the three dynamics—class, race, and gender—have found expression in individual lives and social relationships has formed the agenda for a variety of critical studies on gender and schooling, work that is only beginning" (p. 57). This is a difficult and complex process, for the intersections of these experiences are always historically and socially located. Therefore, any theorization about the politics of knowledge or identity must write against tendencies to essentialize race, class, and gender (Luke & Gore, 1992, p. 7).

Further, the third wave of feminism demands self-reflexivity. It has utilized what was learned from the earlier feminist work for an understanding of the situatedness of gender relations and knowledge within the larger context of disciplinary power. In some ways, this has been marked by a turn toward a poststructural analysis: Third wave feminism has analyzed its own effort to promote essentialized understandings of gender relations or singular truths (Gore, 1993). It has also theorized Foucault's knowledge/power nexus in gendered terms and the deconstruction of the normative subject, of the taken-for-granted historical, social, theoretical, and linguistic structures (Luke & Gore, 1992). Yet although third wave feminism has taken a self-reflexive turn, it would be a mistake to relocate it solely within a poststructural discourse. It continues to embrace the subject, albeit with caution and critique, and searches for ways to ground an antifoundational epistemology in understandings of embodied identities, differences, historicities, and multiple narratives. In fact, it does not openly espouse an antifoundational epistemology, for fear of relativist thinking and loss of responsibility. As Nancy Hartsock (1990) argues, an antifoundational epistemology, the denial of the subject, and the refusal of identity can serve to further marginalize already marginalized groups. This feminist position thus reflects a subjective, contextual, particular, and uncertain reading of the texts in material-theoretical lives: "There are no finite answers, no certainties in any one position" (Luke & Gore, 1992, p. 5). In short, it emphasizes the positional or situated nature of knowledge (Haraway, 1988), power, and authority.

Further, because feminism, unlike poststructuralism, has its roots in a political movement to change oppressive practices and beliefs, it moves beyond deconstruction into reconstruction and agency. This is important. In addition to recognizing science and curriculum as political texts and schools as legitimizers of hegemonic ideals, it also recognizes and draws its strength from teachers and students as agents and actors who actively and collectively shape and reshape their own understandings of the world from specific standpoints. The very belief that students and teachers coconstruct knowledge within a politics of location and identity suggests that knowing—knowing science, knowing education, knowing ourselves, knowing others—is historically and politically contextual, and also changeable. These understandings allow for the intersubjective deconstruction of scientific knowledge and for the construction of alternative visions of science and self (Harding, 1986; Smith, 1987).

Some feminist and feminist poststructural thinkers argue that the denial of the complexity of individuals and their social relations—their locations and interactions as gendered, raced, and classed people in a hierarchically constructed sexist, racist, and classist society—constitutes a "truth regime." As Foucault (1980) writes,

> Each society has its regime of truth, its general politics of truth: That is, the types of discourse which it accepts and makes function as true. . . . [Truth] is centered on the form of scientific discourse and the institutions which produce it; it is subject to constant economic and political incitement (the demand for truth, as much for economic production as for political power); it is the object, under diverse forms, of immense diffusion and consumption (circulating through apparatuses of education and information whose extent is relatively broad in the social body, not withstanding certain strict limitations); it is produced and transmitted under the control, dominant if not exclusive, of a few great political and economic apparatuses (university, army, writing, media); lastly, it is the issue of a whole political debate and social confrontation (ideological struggles). (pp. 131–132)

Impact of Third Wave Feminism on Science Education

This feminist stance holds great opportunities for influence within the science education community, for it questions from a reflexive standpoint the understanding of science as a school subject and as a discipline, students and teachers, and pedagogical interactions. In what follows, I will examine more closely how some emerging third wave feminist thought has shaped work in science education through challenging science as a school subject and as a discipline and through challenging the roles of teachers and students.

Challenging How Science Is Situated as a School Subject. Third wave feminist science education is premised on the belief that science and science education have traditionally been cultures of exclusion that have ignored the multiple narratives, histories, and voices of culturally and politically subordinated groups; it has thus challenged traditional practices in science education on all fronts. Most significantly, its proponents have challenged the representation of science as it is enacted in schools. It is argued that science, like second wave feminism, is not a practice completely separated from other ways of knowing and doing. It is connected to, and influenced by, ways of knowing and doing that permeate every other aspect of life. Similarly, the knowledge produced within the science community is not value-free or independent. Science education—as producing the knowledge of subject matter, academic knowledge—has been used to license cultural differences in order to regulate and define who scientists and science educators are and how they might narrate themselves. From the standpoint of science education, this perspective embraces the subject and searches for ways to ground science teaching and learning in understandings of embodied identities, differences, historicities, and multiple narratives of science and schooling.

In addition to understanding and questioning the nature of science and scientific knowledge, third wave feminist scholars have argued that it is important to make visible the situatedness of science within global ecosystems. This situatedness of science and science education—with their representations of the natural world and their set ways for regulating meaning—is central to understanding how the dynamics of power, privilege, and social desire structure the daily life of society. This demands a close examination of the connection between the production and use of scientific knowledge and authority. In my own work with informal science education at homeless shelters, I argue that it is important for the children to learn to construct science out of their own questions and experiences, even when those experiences challenge societal norms. When their experiences challenge those norms, that difference also needs to be made part of the study (Barton, 1997a). Viewed from another angle, this can be read as science as a social practice with social responsibilities. Howes (1995), for example, has argued that students of genetics must consider the implications that genetic tests such as prenatal testing have for families and for the larger society, in addition to learning the content and process of genetics. Further, Eisenhart, Finkel, and Marion (1996), although not explicitly feminist, have argued that by engaging students in activities that connect participants to communities and science in authentic, useful, and necessary ways, "scientific literacy can be more situated, more relevant, and less exclusive than those advanced under the auspices of the current reform agenda" (p. 289).

Challenging and Situating the Role of Teachers and Students. Third wave feminists also reject the idea that science teachers are simply transmitters of existing configurations of scientific knowledge. Teaching science cannot be reduced to the acquisition or mastery of skills or techniques, but must be defined within a discourse of human agency (Kincheloe, 1993). This means that science teachers must see their work within the larger contexts of culture and community, power and knowledge. Science teaching must be responsible to students for the political and ethical implications that it has for the world it has helped to create, and it must be as infused with analysis and critique as it is with production, refusing to hide behind the modernist claim to objectivity and universal knowledge (Giroux, 1991; Kincheloe, 1993). Teachers help to construct the dynamics of social power through the experiences that they organize and provoke in classrooms. According to Kincheloe (1993), this work is incomplete unless it self-consciously assumes responsibility for its effects in the larger public culture while simultaneously addressing the most profound problems of the societies in which we live. This is a complex idea, but in the case of science education it forces a critical examination of the specific institutional setting in which this teaching-learning takes place. It requires self-reflexivity regarding the particular identities of the teacher and students who collectively undertake this activity and an awareness of how science is negotiated in these settings.

Osborne's (1997) research into the role and knowledge of a teacher illustrates how teachers actively shape relationships around power and knowledge. She develops the argument that a teacher's practice reflects both articulated and unarticulated knowledge and that the practice of teaching inherently involves learning. The knowledge base of teachers is both the foundation on which they are able to teach and also a vehicle through which they are able to learn; through teaching, teachers come to question their knowledge. Such an articulation of theories of teacher knowledge and learning involves an extension and evolution of previous research through the incorporation of ideas derived from feminist and critical theorists. In her work, she suggests that such knowledge, constructed from a teacher's prior experiences, is only partially applicable to particular situations in the classroom (Osborne, 1997). In her vision of the classroom environment and of responsive pedagogy, both are interactive: Because students do not share the knowledge, experiences, or values of the teacher, the classroom becomes a testing ground in which these are reassessed (Osborne, 1997). "Through teaching we are forced to articulate and act upon our values and beliefs in a context different from the ones in which they were formed. In doing this, our values and beliefs are altered because of this new context and through the act of articulation and the self-awareness this entails" (Osborne, in press).

Finally, third wave feminist studies in science education have argued that science teaching is political and activist (WISE, 1996). It is so because of "the researcher's/teacher's critical position and participation in the process of doing research and teaching, and because of the acknowledged subjective movement towards change as a consequence of research and teaching" (p. 3). This kind of feminist thinking challenges the dichotomy between research and action (Harding, 1987). According to WISE (1996), activist science education includes the following characteristics: exploring the ideologies that justify power inequalities, breaking silences, disrupting power relations, daring to decenter science, articulating what is possible and constructing different realities, and experimenting with alternative ways of learning and knowing (p. 3).

Taken together, these main points in feminist research in science education indicate that if all students are to participate in science in genuine ways, science education needs to be re-created so that teachers and students can collaboratively create and analyze science and its role in their lives. Teachers need to help students analyze the role of science in society and in their personal lives, the ways in which scientific knowledge has been constructed through specific political agendas, and the intersections of power and knowledge both inside and outside the community of scientists. Teachers need to help students create new and different representations of science that are inclusive of students' entire lives, and they need to help them interrogate and politicize the intersections of and contradictions between their lives and traditional representations of science.

In the remainder of this book, I chronicle my own attempts to weave this kind of third wave feminist thinking and action—as it has been informed by earlier feminist work—in the community college setting. As a teacher and a researcher, I draw heavily from third wave feminism (and, in particular, from feminist poststructuralism), and from examinations of how this theoretical lens illuminates situated under-standings or positionality, to invent new ideas about science for all, especially as that phrase applies to my students—most of whom express an intense alienation from formal schooling and many of whom repre-sent demographic groups underrepresented in the sciences (racial and ethnic minorities, women, students low on the socioeconomic ladder).

2

Positionality and the Politics of Feminist Teacher Research

Although extremely tired, I did not sleep well last night. I never sleep well the night before the semester starts, as a student or a teacher. All night the same questions kept reemerging in my thoughts: How would my class respond to my nontraditional science and teaching beliefs, actions, and decisions? Would I find ways to connect with my students? Would I help them to understand science and themselves in critical yet accepting ways, or would I simply facilitate and perpetuate status quo ideas about what it means to know and do science, and about who can do science? Could I face another semester of studying my teaching—taping classes, transcribing tapes, interviewing students, keeping a teaching journal, and responding to student journals? These activities consume all of my energy, physically and psychologically. Would my department chair in chemistry catch wind of the changes I have made in the introductory curriculum, against his explicit requests? Would I get fired? Would my students want me to be fired? Would my feminist politics silence my students or provide a space for their ideas to be heard?

Even though class did not start until 6 o'clock in the evening, I drove to the college early to pick up my class list; I wanted to learn as much about the students as I could before class started. Unfortunately, the class list never contains much information—the name of the student and the student number, gender, home phone number, college major, and year in school. The list indicates that there are 15 women and 6 men enrolled in my section with declared majors in occupational or physical therapy, although there are a few premedical, engineering, and bioscience majors, and a small mix of nonscience majors: English, theater, and business. Based on past experience, I expect that most of these students are returning to school after a long absence. For some, it will be the first attempt at college; for others, simply a change in career. Some students will be young and fresh out of high school, but there probably will not be many of these, because this is an evening course, which primarily attracts "nontraditional" students.

My list indicated that there are no chemistry majors in my course this summer—this means that most students are taking chemistry because their majors require it. If this group is anything like last semester's section, only a handful of the 21 students will be looking forward to learning chemistry. Tonight most students will probably tell me that they are either nervous about, not smart enough to, or simply uninterested in studying chemistry. Most will come with the expectation that I will lecture, at a quick pace, about the multitude of facts, theories, and laws embalmed in their texts. Most will also come with the expectation that memorizing a multitude of facts, theories, and laws is what constitutes learning chemistry.

As I continued to study my class list, there was a knock at my office door. It is really not "my office"—I share it with four other women faculty. We have only one desk, one book case, and one file cabinet, but somehow we get everything to fit. Since I was the only one in the office at the time, I put down my class list, scooted my hard wooden chair back along the scratched linoleum floor, stumbled around a pile of books and a box of lab goggles, test tubes, and beakers, and opened the door.

At the door stood an older man with short, gray, thinning hair and glasses at the tip of his long, thin nose. He wondered out loud (and, I assumed, to me, since no one else was in the hall and he did knock at my door) if the students in my chemistry class last semester were smart. Surprised by his comment, I began to tell him about how thoughtful and insightful my spring semester students were (I chose not to describe my students as "smart" because I was and am unsure of its meaning in the context of learning chemistry). He looked me square in the eyes and said he was amazed that all my chemistry students achieved "top grades" when his students were barely passing. I then realized that he was responding to the students' grades from the previous semester, which I had posted on the door. Even though not all of my students received "top grades," I chose not to argue, but instead to explain again how thoughtful and insightful my students were. Interrupting me, he made a semi-audible comment about grade inflation and stomped off down the hall.

As I closed the door, stumbled over the same piles of stuff, and plopped my body back into the chair, which now felt harder than ever, my concentration was shattered. I was angry: angry that I had to defend my students and their integrity against this stranger, angry that I had to be nervous when I gave more than one 4.0 in my class, and angry that I was and am teaching in a department that seems to value impossible exams and student failure. Even if I do succeed in helping students create a place for their voices in science in the space of our classroom, I wonder what good it really does, and what happens when they leave my class for other science classes, for their jobs, and for their families.

Even though I would like to think that tonight, the students and I will begin to create a place in our little classroom for our ideas about science, a shelter from the ever present influence of the powerful institution of science and of the hierarchical structure of education and society, I know that it is impossible. I know that everything we say and do in our class has been inscribed, at least partially, by the innermost workings of science, education, and society, and all of their associated power arrangements that are emblazoned in our hearts and souls. I know that to shake those power arrangements, to challenge them, is what we must do if we are to construct a liberatory teaching and learning setting, but in order to do this we must be aware of where, how, and why those power arrangements exist. We must be aware of how we all participate in and facilitate relationships of power, privilege, and oppression with each other and with science. This is a difficult and complex process, given that much of my thinking, and most likely the thinking of my students, has been, and will be, guided by a master narrative we neither singly wrote, nor completely profit from, but have learned to call our own. (Teaching journal, June 13, 1994)

LEARNING TO QUESTION "SCIENCE FOR ALL"

This book grew out of my attempts as an educator and a scientist to construct a liberatory and inclusive science education with my students. As reflected in my journal entry and in Chapter 1, there are contradictions and dilemmas endemic to "teaching science to all students" (AAAS, 1989). What does it mean to teach science to a diverse class when the science itself embodies only one way of understanding the world? What does it mean to value the ideas of all students when the teacher-student and the scientist-nonscientist relationships are built on hierarchical power arrangements in which the teacher/scientist is considered the knowledge giver, and the student/nonscientist, the knowledge receiver? What does it mean to create mutual meaning among teachers and students when the discourses of science and education do not include the complexity of students' and teachers' lives, gendered, raced, and classed as they are? What does it mean to construct inclusive relationships in science? In short, what does it mean to teach to all students a science that embraces rather than marginalizes multiple standpoints and experiences?

I have not always struggled with these sorts of questions. I have not always believed that schools are places of student resistance or that teachers and students are active agents in constructing and promoting race, class, and gender inequalities. I have not always believed that science is, by its very nature, subjective or that it holds possibilities to be excluding in its practices and content. I have not always believed that students and teachers cooperatively construct knowledge about what it means to know and do science and who can do science. Further, I have not always believed that this knowledge is inherently political and permeated and bound by the power arrangements (and their implied set of rules and expectations) that are active in the classroom.

No, I used to believe that schools and science were authentic meritocracies, inherently good institutions designed to promote, and to accept nothing short of, social justice and human equality. I used to believe that school and science were always right, and that explicitly challenging science or school—to search for alternative visions of science or of the self in science—was wrong. When my wants, needs, and beliefs were in contrast with either school or science, then it was my ideas that were somehow faulty; and when my wants, needs, and beliefs were aligned with school or science, then they were somehow right.

My ideas about school, science, teaching, and learning are not all my own invention. Growing up in a particular culture, I learned to embrace a set of beliefs and biases that shaped and molded my lived experiences (Britzman, 1991). During my life, I have come to know the world from the perspective of a white, middle-class woman. I have learned to participate in a particular set of grand narratives (Gore, 1993), and have learned to work and speak in a particular way within historically and socially determined relations of power. I have learned to live within the contradictions that these grand narratives have created for me in science class—an area of study I learned to love and to hate—as early as childhood:

> Today me, Cathy, and Pru had our tootsie toe warmer sale and no one came to buy them. I AM SO MAD! Number one: They are really cool inventions we made that really do keep your feet warm and are comfy. Number two: We spent forever sewing them and Pru kept bossing us so that they looked good. Number three: We even invented a way to make them look like they were packaged at the store with the plastic baggies and cardboard and stuff. And they were only 10¢. I am so mad, but next time we decided that we would just sell flowers. At least that way some people will stop. (Personal diary from my childhood)

This journal entry locates me with two of my four sisters in a small working- and middle-class New England town where we spent most of our time growing up. We lived on one of the main roads in town, and my sisters and I took advantage of the busy street by having various sales to make a few bucks. We mostly sold flowers that we had picked from our neighbors' field, but sometimes we got adventurous and tried to invent something new to sell. In this case, it was Tootsie Toe Warmers. We were sure we had a winner. After all, they did not have all the hassles of slippers. Tootsie Toe Warmers could be kept on the feet while shoes were worn, for example. And, they kept toes warm, a place on our bodies which happened to get cold the easiest and the fastest.

A Tootsie Toe Warmer is actually a rather simple yet creative invention (or so we thought). We sewed a piece of material (by hand) so it looked like a partial sock. Then we attached an elastic band that would wrap around the ankle to keep the Tootsie Toe Warmer on the foot. Then we put each pair in a plastic baggie, and stapled it shut with a piece of cardboard on which we wrote "Tootsie Toe Warmers" along with directions on how to use them and wash them. We even made different sizes (small, medium, and large).

My parents seemed to enjoy our entrepreneurial spirit, in part I think because they wanted to instill in us the belief that we could do anything as long as we put our minds to it. Yet this kind of encouragement to explore, experiment, and invent was not always forthcoming in school, and, in fact, was often withheld within school science:

> I had learned in science class earlier in the year that it was not safe to smell a bottle with chemicals in it because it could kill you or at least burn your nose hairs, and that the proper technique was to waft the bottle odors by your nose with your hand. In our class, we had to make an invention, and I thought that a neat and needed invention would be to have a nose with a chemical detector in it. I

thought it would be the coolest project. So, I made a nose out of plaster of Paris and glued some hair by the nostrils. This hair was the chemical detector ends. Attached to the nose was a piece of chalk and a piece of paper. This was to print out the list of chemicals that the nose smelled. All you had to do was put the nose over the bottle of chemicals in question, and it would print out the chemicals. I was so proud of my project, and I didn't even care when the class laughed because it was kind of funny. Anyway, my teacher gave me a C- because it was not realistic and did not really work. [Despite the fact that the same teacher gave Vic an A+ when his project—a telephone TV where you could see the person you were talking to—was not realistic and did not really work. And, he only drew a picture of his. I made a model!]. (Memory from seventh grade)

My stories of this age construct a gendered, yet gender-questioning, existence. In my seventh-grade science class, I learned the hard way to accept the roles and expectations for girls and science. I learned that neither my voice nor my ideas counted. When I tried to express an interest for and creativity in chemistry, I was punished by my teacher for not being realistic, whereas Vic was praised for the same thing. By the time I was a teenager, I knew that being a woman meant finding common ground amid contradiction. My teachers, textbooks, and class lessons were telling me that women were not scientists. Yet my love of exploring and theorizing about my world, which I was encouraged to do at home and occasionally at school, told me that I could and should be a scientist. That I found ways to combine these mixed messages was evident in my everyday activities and inventions. For example, the Tootsie Toe Warmers combined my desire to see that everyone's feet stayed warm and my knowledge of sewing with inventiveness and business. My nose-shaped chemical detector grew out of my need to keep the body safe and to help clean the air and was mixed with my interest in invention and analysis.

Today I fed:
    Fruit fly group A: two slices of banana
    Fruit fly group B: one slice of banana mixed with one aspirin
    Fruit fly group C: one-half slices of banana mixed with two aspirin
    Fruit fly group D: two aspirin.
    I removed one fruit fly from each group and analyzed them under the microscope and found that:

Group A: looked normal

Group B: looked normal

Group C: looked sick. I think it was smaller than the normal ones.

Group D: was dead before I could kill it to examine it. I think it died from the aspirin. (Science project notebook, Mr. Bolin's 10th-grade biology class)

This science notebook entry places me in the grand narrative of a positivistic science. It portrays me as a high school student successfully learning how to engage in the discourse and practice of science. I learned to set up controlled, objective experiments. In the name of science, I killed fruit flies—by starvation or intoxication through diet regulation (I never figured out which) and by suffocation—to observe them more accurately under the microscope. I felt sad about the poor little fruit flies, but I was awarded for these efforts at school, district, and state science fairs.

I know that in my own experiences, the voice that I developed with my sisters to invent Tootsie Toe Warmers, find frogs, or build go-carts was not a voice I used in school. No, I used another voice. I spoke the language of the science books we were given. I spoke without emotion, without feeling. In science class and at science fairs, I talked about fruit flies dying from aspirin; at home I talked about the poor little flies not receiving decent meals. Science was a difficult topic in which only serious, intellectual students engaged. That was the voice I needed to assume. In biology I never talked about our nature walks at home; in physics I never talked about our go-carts; in chemistry I never talked how I made sense of the composition of the world. That would be immature and unscientific, for these ideas were grounded in my play experiences, not on rigorous intellectual study. My first science voice, the one I constructed at home and sometimes at school, sank away into silence.

As I gained experience in science, both in school and then in industry, I refined my acquired science voice. I spoke from a distance: I spoke as if scientific knowledge was real and objective, free of personal or public bias and values. I spoke as if the world of science made more sense than my world of experience. I learned to develop an empirical worldview and to understand science in a rather strict positivist fashion. I was taught to believe that in order to obtain objective knowledge, I could separate myself from my object of study. To mention or even to think that I, the human observer, could be an agent who studies and influences, and that my scientific ideas were wrapped up in and exhibited cultural, social, political, and economic values was absurd. Despite this conflict of identity, I continued to explore the domain of traditional science, for it promised to hold the answers. It certainly held the power.

Without my revisiting my entire life history, it is pretty clear how my role as science teacher and researcher in science education is situated historically and socially. My teaching and research are, by their nature, social practices that can only be understood through considerations of history, politics, power, and culture (Giroux, 1994, p. 280). As Henry Giroux (1994) wrote:

> If educators are to take seriously the challenge of cultural studies, particularly its insistence on generating new questions, models, and contexts in order to address the central and most urgent dilemmas in our age, they must critically address the politics of their own location. This means understanding not only the ways in which the institutions of higher education play their part in shaping the work we do with students, but also the ways in which our vocation as educators supports, challenges, or subverts institutional practices that are at odds with democratic processes and the hopes and opportunities we provide for the nation's youth. (pp. 278–279)

Third wave feminism constantly questions how relationships and knowledge are situated within webs of knowledge and power. As a third wave feminist educator, I feel that it is necessary to understand science teaching and learning in their contexts. Just a quick reflection on my own understandings of school and science illustrates situated knowledge well. It also illustrates how any explorations, analyses, or attempts to create science for all in my classroom are embedded in my own situational understandings of science, knowledge, and power, in my own history and identity. I believe that the positional nature of science teaching and learning must be explored in order to develop deep and contextual understandings of what it means to teach science for all. Reflexively, it is also important to understand how a teacher's understanding of the positional nature of teaching and learning can open possibilities for a more liberatory education in science for all students. These two intertwined issues, deeply rooted in the feminist attempt to understand the situatedness of gender relations and knowledge within the larger context of disciplinary power, guide the teaching, researching, and writings in this book. In what follows, I develop the idea of positionality, its potential role in science teaching and learning and in teacher research. I also use my situated role as a teacher-researcher who is developing understanding of the positional nature of teaching and learning to explore possibilities for a more liberatory education in science for all students.

POSITIONALITY

Positionality as Relational

Positionality is the "knower's specific position in any context as defined by gender, race, class, and other socially significant dimensions" (Maher & Tetreault, 1994, p. 22). It locates teachers, researchers, and students and their interpretations and analysis of what happens in classrooms within multiple ideological positions. This kind of thinking about what happens in classrooms is important because it highlights how each person's positionality influences the social construction of knowledge. It emphasizes the relational or situated nature of knowledge (Haraway, 1988). It also implies the relational or situated nature of power and authority in the classroom (Maher & Tetreault, 1993, 1994). Positionality is a kind of metaknowledge locating the self in relation to the other within social structures, such as the classroom, that re-create and mediate those relationships (Maher & Tetreault, 1994, p. 202). For example, as Maher and Tetreault (1994) described in their study of feminist classrooms:

> [Positionality] has made an important difference in our study, for example, whether teachers and students were male or female, white or African-American, heterosexual or lesbian. And those differences have varied according to history, religion, experiences, and "cultural practices" that brought participants to each classroom and positioned them there. (p. 22)

> In sum, exploring the meanings of positionality . . . entails basic challenges to our conventional notions of communication and knowledge construction. In these groups, we saw how knowledge could emerge from the acknowledgment of deep positional differences. The layers of language, emotion, and conflicting meaning implicit in different positions can be plumbed, raised to the surface and explored. (p. 200)

Maher and Tetreault argue that each person is "positioned" by an individual set of multiple identities and lived experiences, and that students and teachers bring this to the classroom. Yet these labels that dissect and categorize the full set of experiences through which each individual comes to know the world are not so easily pulled apart.

Positionality as Dynamic

Positionality is not static. Although definitions or labels are sometimes used to describe one's position, the terms that we use to describe ourselves are "highly unstable since the culturally generated meaning and understandings articulated to these terms continually undergo personal and social transformation" (Orner, 1992, p. 74). The inability to fix meanings to these labels is a powerful means through which we can denaturalize ourselves and embrace change. The very idea that we are positioned in the classroom or in any other context by our experiences argues against pinpointing any singular source of understanding or spaces for theorizing.

Positionality as Political

Positionality is also political, because it refers to the relational space that people occupy within a set of sociopolitical relationships (Alcoff, 1988; Harding, 1986, 1991; hooks, 1990; Maher & Tetreault, 1993, 1994). For example, Maher and Tetreault (1994) and the teachers in their study used positionality as a framework for understanding how students "fashioned" ideas in terms of race, class, gender, and sexuality. Teaching and researching practices can also be understood through the ways in which one's life experiences shape assumptions, beliefs, values, and, ultimately, practice. This practice of deconstruction can be particularly helpful in bringing to the surface the ways in which embedded privilege or oppression, power and control, is used to promote or break down seemingly natural practices or beliefs in a society. In this sense, positionality underscores the relationships between power, culture, knowledge, authority, teaching, and learning.

These relational, shifting, and political qualities of positionality connect this concept to teaching and learning in powerful ways. Teachers make decisions based on their knowledge of subject matter, students, and pedagogy and how they interact. In a progressive framework, this means understanding how knowledge, students, and teaching practice interact. Positionality provides a powerful lens through which to view the interactions between these three things, because it provides a standpoint from which to explore the ideological foundations of school and science as well as the values and beliefs that students and teachers bring to school. It also provides a lens for understanding the ways in which those values and beliefs interact with "required curriculum and school practices" and for acknowledging the political dimensions of education and the different methods that teachers and students have "to exercise power [over] their own lives, and especially over the conditions of knowledge production and acquisition" (Giroux, 1991, p. 50). For example, as a science teacher interested in helping students become "liberated from science," it is important for me to understand teaching and learning science in the context of my own and my students' lives: In what ways have my students' experiences as raced, classed, and gendered people influenced their engagements in science and their possible futures with science? How did the students' positionalities shape the way they learned science in my classroom or the way they interacted with me or with each other? This lens of positionality, I believe, can help to uncover assumptions that I used uncritically, and perhaps unknowingly, in my teaching—assumptions about what science is, who can do science, what it means to teach and learn across race, class, and gender.

POSITIONALITY AND FEMINIST SCIENCE TEACHER RESEARCH

Positionality plays a key role in the development of a feminist science education. Knowledge, perspective, and experience are created in historical, political, and cultural contexts and within power relationships. For teachers to make sense of multiple students' voices in class at any given moment, they need to locate the ways in which the multiple subjectivities present in class interact and contradict. Reading classroom interaction and action through the lens of positionality foregrounds how beliefs, values, ideology, power, and knowledge become intertwined in the classroom. To get into positionality and feminist science teaching, I need to bring you into my story.

Positioning My Story: Teaching at Ashton Community College

The teaching I write about in this book occurred in the chemistry program at Ashton Community College. This is a two-year community college located in downtown Ashton, a midsize city in the Midwest. Sandwiched between the state capital district and low-income housing, the college serves a diverse population. Its stated mission is to serve the urban community's educational needs. It boasts of its efforts to reach out to the working community through its day, evening, and weekend programs as well as its off-campus teaching locations. Most of my teaching occurred at an extension site located in one of the Ashton high schools, only 3 miles from Ashton's main campus. The college has several other extension sites, some of which are located as many as 60 miles away from the main campus.

The administrators at the community college offer several reasons for the existence of the extension sites. First, extension sites make access to the physical location of school easier for the students. Because many students at Ashton are also part- or full-time workers and parents, long-distance travel is often out of the question. Second, because most of the extension schools are located in high schools or community centers, they may not be as intimidating as a college setting. This is an important issue because many of Ashton's students are returning to school after long and possibly alienating absences from formal schooling. The third reason is the limited classroom space on Ashton's campus. The extension sites accommodate the college's overflow needs.

Most of the students in the evening extension program enroll in chemistry to meet official program requirements. This, however, is not the only concern to influence their choice of enrolling in the extension site chemistry course. Several students in my extension courses selected my particular section of chemistry because it was an evening course and therefore fit better with their work and family schedules. Other students took the course at the extension site because they felt intimidated taking a course at the college. Many believed that they would be in a smaller class at the extension school. Finally, many of the female students wanted a female instructor, and mine was the only female name in the course catalog for introductory chemistry.

The students' reasons for wanting to take their courses through the Ashton extension program are not surprising. Most of the students were older than the traditional college student (over 25 years of age). Most attended the community college part-time during the evening so they could keep their daytime jobs as secretaries, health care assistants, custodians, factory workers, teachers, librarians, data processors, and cosmetologists. Finally, most had little "formal" educational training beyond high school.

As a feminist teacher, I liked teaching in the Ashton extension program because, like my students, I also liked being "off campus." I liked being away from the authorities. When I taught on campus, I always felt highly self-conscious of my decisions to move away from the more traditional (and expected) classroom practices. When I taught in the extension program, I felt that I had more freedom to explore nontraditional teaching ideas: I was not as worried about the noise level in my room, about the way the tables were arranged, or that I did not locate myself in the front of the room. I also felt more at ease helping the students to critique science. However, there were three major drawbacks to teaching at the extension site. First, there was the lack of available equipment for use in class. Whenever I needed equipment for class, from paper to hot plates, I had to transport it myself from the main campus to the high school. Second, there was an underlying belief that what happened at these extension sites was not as "real" as what happened at the real campus. Third (and this would not have been solved by being in the on-campus chemistry classroom), there was the physical structure and space of the classroom at the extension site. In the front of the classroom was a blackboard and a teacher's workbench-desk, which sat on a raised platform. Spread out through the room were several rows of student benches (which we rearranged in a horseshoe design). There was an empty bulletin board to one side of the room and a counter covered with books and papers on the other. After covering the empty board with our work, we found it removed, at our next class meeting, along with a note in my box stating that this was not our space to use. In the back of the room were locked shelves filled with chemistry lab equipment. Our study of chemistry and our vision of what it means to know and to do chemistry was immediately physically bound. Chemistry occurred inside the walls of academe and science. It required expensive equipment that was to be locked out of the reach of ordinary people. It required a serious, even sullen, atmosphere, and an expert who intellectually and physically could stand above the rest of the class.

This brief introduction to teaching chemistry at Ashton begins to shed some light on just how much feminist science teaching at the community college takes place within the wider cultural and institutional structures of school and science, and on the implications that this has for teaching and learning science. In what follows, I illustrate how these cultural and institutional structures at Ashton, which are typical of many educational institutions, work against feminist and liberatory education through an agenda of rigidity, homogeneity, and control.

For example, although teaching science at Ashton is more flexible than it is at most high schools because there are 2-hour rather than 45-minute blocks for teaching and learning, the structure of the science education at the community college is still rigid. We had prescribed meeting times, locations, textbooks, and homework assignments, with their own predefined grading rubric handed down from the department office. There was a predetermined set of content objectives to be completed along with department-ordered exams and exam dates. Even before our class officially started, before the students or I ever had the chance to express our needs, desires, and fears for an education in science, much of our lives in science and education had already been inscribed. The students and their teacher, all of whom arrived at Ashton from different life circumstances, were expected to passively accept these rigidly defined structures.

There are messages implicit in such rigid structures, one of which centers on the idea of homogeneity in experience, circumstance, and expectation. Predefined knowledge sets and ways in which to introduce, practice, and monitor the development of them is based on the assumptions that all students will assimilate into the culture of science equally and unproblematically; that all students will come to learning science with the same cultural capital; and that all students have the same uses for science. This is supported by a neoconservative society's vision of equity and science's vision of objectivity. The students in my chemistry classes came from diverse backgrounds, ethnically and racially. Although most students were working class, there were a small number of professional students in each class and young students from middle-class families. And so despite our vast differences, we each entered the course equally yet unequally inscribed by the dominant discourses in science and education. It is no wonder to me that when students come to class for the first time, they have certain expectations about science, school, teaching, and learning, all of which are based on positivistic and imperialistic worldviews. These ideas and expectations are not easily erased in the context of school, even when they leave students and teachers feeling uncomfortable or marginalized (Weiler, 1988).

It is within such structural limits that I work hard to challenge the ideas and expectations that are tightly held by the students and promoted by the institutions of science and education. Challenging these ideas is difficult because they permeate everything we say, do, and experience:

> Decolonizing educational practices requires transformations at a number of levels, both within and outside the academy. Curricula and pedagogical transformation had to be accompanied by a broad-based transformation of the culture of the academy, as well as by radical shifts in the relation of the academy to other state and civil institutions. In addition, decolonizing pedagogical practices requires taking seriously the relation between knowledge and learning, on the one hand, and students and teacher experience on the other. In fact the theorization and politicization of experience is imperative if pedagogical practices are to focus on more than the mere management, systemization and consumption of disciplinary knowledge. . . . this pedagogy is an attempt to get students to think critically about their place in relation to the knowledge they gain and to transform their worldview fundamentally by taking the politics of knowledge seriously. (Mohanty, 1994, p. 152)

Pursuing the kind of systematic changes required for a socially transforming education as they are laid out by Mohanty are extremely difficult. Such changes require challenging accepted definitions of school and science, deconstructing an ideology of white, male, middle-class privilege, and establishing purposes and goals for a science education meant for critical consciousness rather than for fact accumulation. This is especially difficult because the very institutions within which we must work have prefabricated obstacles and boundaries such as prescribed texts, syllabi, exams, homework, definitions of science, and definitions of success. We must climb over or break through these obstacles even before class officially begins.

Yet there are at least two more obstacles to realizing the goal of a feminist science class beyond these imposed physical requirements. First, feminist goals appear to be in opposition to the goals of science and education (as they are both currently practiced). Science and education both operate within a positivistic paradigm that acknowledges only one acceptable worldview. This world view is so unproblematically accepted in science education that it is believed to be objective. Second, the multicultural, multiclassed, and multigendered community college setting creates a complex set of interactions inside and outside the classroom between teacher and students, teacher and science, students and science, and students themselves. As Weiler suggests, the difficulty in achieving [feminist] goals in multicultural and mixed-class public school settings becomes obvious through an examination of classroom discourse. In class, teachers and students negotiate meaning through their own set of lived experiences. Yet the question of whose ideas are legitimized through such a negotiation process is difficult to answer because of the multiple and interacting power arrangements in the classroom. "Classroom discourse . . . is never neutral, but is always situated in the context of a socially and historically defined present. Teachers and students use language to assert their own power and to try to create some sense for themselves out of a complex social setting" (Weiler, 1988, pp. 128–129). Thus the possibilities of and obstacles to counterhegemonic teaching in science are complex, shifting, and multiple.

Positionality and Feminist Science Education

This brings me back to the idea of positionality and the role it can play in developing feminist science education. My goals as a feminist teacher-researcher are to try to read subjectivity and to politicize its artifacts. Because positionality highlights the subjective, shifting, and political nature of teaching, the power of positionality in science education lies in part in its ability to promote the examination of teaching in a way that allows one to recognize and make problematic how socially and culturally derived norms for science and teaching drive science teaching and learning. This kind of teacher research promotes the articulation of how gender, race, and class locations shape expectations for normative patterns of behavior (Davidson, 1994). As Kathleen Weiler (1988) wrote:

> Feminist teachers, if they are to work to create a counter-hegemonic teaching, must be conscious of their own gendered, classed and raced subjectivities as they confirm or challenge the lived experiences of their students. This does not mean avoiding or denying conflict, but legitimizing this polyphony of voices and making both our oppression and our power conscious in the discourse of the classroom. (p. 145)

Thus, teacher research provides a "truly emic perspective that makes visible the ways students and teachers together construct knowledge" (Lytle & Cochran-Smith, 1992, p. 448). Teacher research opens up this discourse on positionality because it resists the ingrained belief that teachers are mere transmitters of predesigned knowledge frames and knowledge claims. Teacher research allows teachers and others to view the practice of teaching as an always unfinished and incomplete activity; in science education it creates spaces for teachers to question identity, inherited dogmas, and absolute beliefs and to begin to see themselves in relation to the world around them. Teacher research promotes an inseparable relationship between thinking and acting, as the boundary between feeling and logic begins to fade from the cognitive map (Kincheloe, 1993).

Feminist teacher research and positionality are also brought together through the intertwined feminist intentions of praxis, politics, and activism. In my research and teaching, I want to help my students change the science in their lives and in their classroom. Praxis, according to Lather (1991, pp. 11–12), has two requirements. First, it must be composed of theory relevant to the world nurtured by action in it. Second, there must be an action component that grows out of "practical political grounding." My research, my thinking, and my actions have evolved over time, affecting each other reciprocally, and are shaped by my changing understanding of feminist and poststructural theories, my students, and our changing visions of each other and of science (WISE, 1995). Through viewing my teaching and research as subjective political acts for social change, I am creating a form of transformative feminist praxis. A political commitment in research to change and be changed is a form of feminist praxis because it "encompasses both reflection and action as a form of inquiry that promotes a better, fairer, more humane world" (Miller, 1990, p. 13).

I believe that to come to a greater understanding of how a feminist agenda is lived in the classroom, it is necessary to understand how a teacher's actions and reflections can be informed by underlying assumptions about science and school. When I reflect on what it means to bring a feminist agenda to science education, it became obvious to me that the ways in which I act upon my own feminist teaching agenda are contextually dependent. I make sense of this agenda in connection with my understanding of myself and the world; to the understandings and experiences that my students bring to class, and my interpretation of those experiences; and my beliefs about the content that I teach. Therefore, as a white, female, feminist teacher hoping to construct a liberatory teaching and learning setting, I feel it is important that I understand how my lived experiences have shaped my connected and situated understanding of school, science, and students. My hope is to be able to use this reflexive thought and the subsequently informed actions to move science teaching toward attainment of its liberatory potential. By engaging in a form of teacher research that seeks to challenge and transform traditional assumptions of students and school, I hope to not only push my own practice as a teacher toward more liberatory aims, but also to create new spaces in teacher research for nontraditional voices.

3

Positioning Science Through Oral Histories

As bell hooks (1990) pointed out, choosing the margin as a place of radical resistance creates possibilities for disrupting hegemonic reality because it offers a vantage point outside of mainstream culture from which to interpret the world. What does it mean to create a place of radical resistance or to disrupt hegemonic reality in science class? Can the hegemonic reality be disrupted through productive and meaningful acts of political resistance—in ways that will make science more inclusive? For example, will disrupting hegemonic reality create a science that allows for personally relevant ways of thinking about science? What is required of teachers and students as gendered, classed, and ethnically diverse people if such radical vantage points are to be constructed in science class—inside the walls of the institutions of science and education?

In the previous chapter, I described how positionality highlights the subjective, shifting, and political nature of teaching. Here, I explore my own and my students' attempts to create places of radical resistance in science class—places where competing and intersecting realities, questions, and concerns typically perceived as marginal to science are valued—through "oral history" conversations. To do so, I build on the previous chapter's argument to suggest that one way to utilize these dimensions of positionality in science class is by valuing lived experiences in such a way that competing and intersecting realities, questions, and concerns typically perceived as marginal to science are allowed to intersect with classroom discourse about science and other things.

THE ORAL HISTORIES

As a course requirement, each student in my chemistry class completed an oral history project where he or she was to have an extended conversation with a local community member to learn more about how science, and, in particular, chemistry, influenced her or his life in personal and professional ways. The initial goals for introducing oral histories into chemistry class were to begin to make the practice of chemistry less abstract, to broaden the definition of science with which students came to class, to broaden the definition of chemistry practiced in class, and to connect the theory of the classroom to practice. With these in mind, I encouraged students to select people who were not traditional scientists, so that as a class we could develop a broad understanding of what science is and of what it means to be a scientist. The students were required to report on their conversations, although there were no restrictions placed on the content of them other than finding out how the interviewees thought about science. Because, however, many of the oral histories involved people who were not traditional scientists, our class talked a great deal about things other than traditional science. Students reported on "disillusioned" scientists, feminist science teachers, and child care providers. These reports exposed the subjective and positional nature of knowing science and created spaces for the students in my class and for me in which to understand our own positional understanding about science and the self-in-science. The creation of these spaces pushed against the boundaries of Western science; we began to reposition ourselves in science. In what follows, I share excerpts from four class conversations that reflect how the students began to reread science and their experiences in science through their lives. Each of the first three touches on a different theme (the human element, elitism, and the political dimensions of science) and how that theme broadened and shaped our spaces; the fourth story weaves the themes together.

SHELLIE'S ORAL HISTORY: LISA KARMS AND THE HUMAN ELEMENT IN SCIENCE

During the 5th week of the spring semester, Shellie, a young mother of two children, presented her oral history project. Her interviewee was Lisa Karms, a local cancer researcher. Shellie had enrolled in this course after a ten-year hiatus from school. She had returned part-time to study counseling, yet maintained her full-time job as a receptionist for a local doctor to help her family "make ends meet." Chemistry was "low" on her "list of things to do" but she enrolled in the course immediately upon her return to school to "get the requirement out of the way." Shellie felt that the school was "justified in making her take chemistry" as part of her program. However, she was extremely vocal about her dislike of and perceived inaptitude in the study of chemistry.

Shellie's report emphasized the "human element" in doing science. First, she made her own feelings and those of her interviewee's central to her presentation. She talked about how her feelings of intimidation and dread brought on by having to talk with a person who was "much brighter in science than she was" were unfounded because Lisa Karms was "personable, down-to-earth, and not at all like a scientist." Lisa Karms even made her "kind of excited about science" because even though Lisa admitted that she had had a hard time with chemistry in school, and sometimes an even harder time being the only woman in her lab, "it was worth it when you figured out something new and could share it with other people and help them to understand too." Furthermore, although Shellie did describe Lisa's cancer research, she focused primarily on Lisa's feelings and experiences: Lisa's belief that her work was slow and tedious, the frustrations she felt as a scientist because "if you have not gotten your years in or your time in, you probably don't know as much as the rest of us," her dissatisfaction with the lack of free time outside of science (a condition of being recognized as a competent and dedicated scientist), and the self-consciousness that Lisa felt as a "woman in white, male-dominated science." Second, Shellie presented Lisa's experiences of being disillusioned with science because the science itself lacked "humanness":

> One thing [Lisa] said when I really picked on her . . . she was very disillusioned with science. She said the hardest part for her was there didn't seem to be a holistic kind of science, it was broken down into such small units that it didn't seem to have any humanness to it. What she is doing now, she said that she feels comfortable because she is looking at the whole. She is studying something that she feels is very useful.

Shellie's provocative statements regarding the "human element" and science sparked other student responses and questions in the discussion that followed her report. John, an older student who works full-time delivering oxygen equipment to people with respiratory ailments, saw the need for the human element in his employment in the health care industry:

> Okay, well I've been dealing with respiratory therapy for the past 4½ years and it's all an interrelated thing. It's a human-related thing, and anything technical, it is more or less just in my head.

But, in relating with the people, I eliminate the technical part and rely on a bedside manner, you know, the human element is every-thing. And the science part of it, it's really all in here (he gestures toward his head). It's just brought out in how I do my job, but it's never related to the people. Okay, that's one part of it, but now as I was just thinking about it, I used to work in a chrome plate factory, and I worked as a lab assistant and that was a really neat job. The thing about it that was neat was that they used electrically charged probes down in a solution to chrome plate parts and stuff. And come to think about it up until recently, how much that relates to what we are doing and how I used to mix chemicals in the lab, and we dealt with a lot of nasty stuff. Six months on the job and I quit. There was no human element, but, I got to learn how the electrical aspects of it works, chrome bonding to metal, and I don't really remember, it has been quite a while but it was a nasty job. It was dangerous. . . . Most of the people are elderly, and they need oxy-gen for their heart, and they don't understand how the machine brings oxygen.

Shellie asked John if a lot of the older patients were scared of the machines, to which he replied:

At first, they are afraid to lay down and go to sleep even though it is perfectly safe. Some people ask, they want to know what's going on, how is this really helping? And, what's going on with their lungs and their heart. And most people don't ask, they just want to make sure that you are there, that you are doing your job, and they appreciate your work.

From previous class conversations, I knew that John enjoyed his work in home health care—he was in a respiratory therapy certification program at the community college so that he would have the credentials for more responsibility at work. Did John find the human element an essential part of his respiratory work? Was it the lack of the human element that drove him away from his work at the chrome plate factory? Connecting people and their everyday struggles and activities to science and using science to alleviate struggles is how John defines the human element in science.

Other students responded to the concept of the human element in different ways. Gene, a 1st-year physical science teacher, believed that the human element was needed in schools through "doing science":

If you think about what scientists do, scientists try to solve problems to make life better for you and for me. I know that is debatable though, but what I want to point out is that sometimes the science that scientists do and science in the classroom can be different. Sometimes in class we don't do the experiments that scientists do, and so the human element can be removed easily. Unless we are using our hands and our minds like scientists while we are in class by exploring, doing some hands-on science, then it will be hard for the human element to be there.

Laurie, also an older student, who works as a data processor, went beyond personal action and challenged the entire scientific enterprise:

I just interviewed my person and he is a full professor and he does a lot of research. He is in charge of a collaborative research team, and I was really disillusioned in terms of the human element with some of the things that he said. He is doing research related to genes and cancer and things like that. I thought that would be rewarding enough, and that would come out in the interview, but he talked about the monetary aspects and that bothered me because he said that society does not place enough value on those things. He said we pay people in sports and performing arts, we have all this money, but we are not paying people in research, and that kind of bothered me . . . because what I thought what would come up in our conversation was the human aspects of his work, but it was more of the idea that this was valuable to society and you should pay us more. You hear sometimes that the doctors are only in it for the money, and then you interview somebody like this and it makes you wonder.

Laurie, John, and Gene were concerned about engagement in science for a purpose: to make life better for people. For Laurie and John, science is an intentional and powerful activity because it shapes lives. Consequently, it was important for these two students to make the human connections central to thinking and doing science. Further, Laurie was bothered by the clinical researcher who wanted to do science for recognition and money. She expected a deeper and more personal human involvement in and attachment to science and an overriding sense of caring about its ultimate uses. John was bothered by an indirect connection between science and human life. These comments were powerful beginnings to a critique of science because they questioned the motives for, as well as ethical implications of, doing certain kinds of science.

The students' responses to Shellie's presentation echoed Lisa Karms's feelings of disillusionment and her desire to explore the human element in science. The students connected with the Lisa Karms conversation on a personal level. Because that presentation provided opportunities for connections to feelings of disillusionment, the students, in some ways, also had a safer space to "stand up to" those feelings of disillusionment created by science. The conversation validated the students' experiences and, in particular, those that did not neatly fit into the mold of the typical scientist. As a result, their experiences outside of science both physically and ideologically repositioned science in our class so that it became a something to be challenged rather than an impenetrable force. In some ways, this evening's class was a turning point because Lisa's disillusionment with science and her need to find a human piece to science created a space in which the students could speak critically of their connections with and disconnections from science. Her experiences as a "real scientist" were not the glorious and trouble-free "I love science" experiences propagated in science education.

Reflecting on this conversation, I also learned more about how positionality can contribute to liberatory education. As many of the students and I talked about ourselves and about science, we formulated new ideas about who we were in science class, what we knew and what we wanted to know, and where we fit. We found spaces in our conversation in which to value our lived experiences, even those that were not validated by traditional science. This kind of talking and thinking in science class works to help students construct new meaning and relationships with and in science.

LAURIE'S ORAL HISTORY: KURT PHILLIPS AND
THE ELITISM OF WESTERN SCIENCE

Laurie presented her oral history during the class following Shellie's presentation. She was not completely happy in her current position because she felt she was not respected. For example, about 1 year before enrolling in this chemistry class, she had almost lost her job as a result of her pregnancy. She was told that it would have been too expensive for the company to offer her a 6-week maternity leave. She was able to keep her job when she agreed to a shortened maternity leave. Laurie, like Shellie, had enrolled in a part-time evening program at the college.

Her goal was to eventually attend optometry school and to work more closely with people.

Laurie introduced her oral history candidate, Dr. Phillips, a clinical chemistry researcher, by sharing his credentials with the class. The class had been warned about Dr. Phillips during the conversation that had followed Shellie's report when Laurie shared with the class that she had been disillusioned with clinical research practice after talking with Dr. Phillips. To her .dismay, she learned that foremost on Dr. Phillips's mind was, rather than helping humanity, finding a salary commensurate with his perceived self-worth. So the class was ready when Laurie only briefly described Dr. Phillips's accomplishments in the medical research profession, such as his helping to isolate the gene involved in severe mental retardation or his opinion on "what kinds of science are most objective," so she could focus on his attitude toward medicine, research, money, and the need for "more prestige in and respect for science." As Laurie told the class:

> When I asked Dr. Phillips if there was anything he would change about chemistry, he said that he would increase the monetary compensation for professors of chemistry. Professors of chemistry often are directly involved in valuable research which can have a direct impact on health and human lives. He feels that society's values are warped, as we reward professional athletes and national performers and actors with millions of dollars in compensation for their professions.
>
> And when I asked him if he felt if one needed a given aptitude for chemistry, he said that he did not feel that chemistry was at all a difficult subject. He did not elaborate, but he gave me the subtle impression that he did not really understand why one would think chemistry is difficult, as it is a "way of life" for him. He seemed so stuck on himself, so unaware that just because he may have some insight into chemistry doesn't mean that everyone does. I would never dare tell him how hard this stuff is to comprehend sometimes.
>
> Finally, when I asked him what his greatest sacrifice was for having chosen chemistry as a career, he said that it was the lack of money during the period he was getting his doctorate degree in chemistry. Many of his peers were able to purchase things he was not able to during the time he was pursuing his PhD.

The ideas that Laurie shared about Dr. Phillips were in stark contrast to Shellie's report on Lisa Karms. Lisa talked about needing to bring in the human element; Dr. Phillips talked about needing to re-move human bias. Lisa talked about finding a way to study science by looking across large systems; Dr. Phillips talked about the importance of searching for new things at the molecular level. Lisa talked about how she understood that chemistry is a difficult topic and how she has even had problems understanding it herself; Dr. Phillips talked about how easy chemistry was and how he had never had problems with it, even in high school. Lisa talked about how research required funding and how the whole funding process reminded her of the political nature of science. Dr. Phillips, although mentioning that research required fund-ing, had emphasized that he deserved more money. Finally, Lisa ex-pressed frustration with the difficulties she had had as a woman in this very male-dominated profession, whereas Dr. Phillips talked about how "anyone" could do science if determined enough and about how the system is set up to ensure that only "quality" work survives.

Laurie's presentation opened the door for the students to build on their emerging analysis of science. The first focus of critique had been on the human element in science. The discussion of Dr. Phillips led the students into "elitist attitudes." During Shellie's presentation on Lisa Karms, the theme of personal connections and disillusion with science had emerged in Laurie's report. In line with student responses in the conversation that followed Shellie's presentation, Laurie, Gwen, and Shellie appeared to be concerned with engaging in science for purpose-ful reasons. They all had difficulties with Dr. Phillips's attitude about money and prestige in science and the "elitism" connected to those ideas:

> LAURIE: Like I said, I did not really enjoy talking with Dr. Phillips. He seemed so stuck on himself. He seemed to care a whole lot about things that were very different from what I care about. As I said the other day, all he talked about was money, money, money, and it was as if nothing else in science mat-tered to him. Well, he did mention some stuff related to the gene for mental retardation, but he kept coming back to the money thing. I guess, as much as I do not want to believe it, some people are in it for only the money.
>
> SHELLIE: He was so much different than Lisa Karms. I really en-joyed talking with Lisa, I would like to talk with her again.
>
> TEACHER: What do you mean, he was different? Were there ideas that specifically stuck out to you?
>
> SHELLIE: The money, and how stuck on himself he was. Lisa

seemed more interested in helping people. Not that Laurie's person didn't, he was just more concerned with his career.

GWEN: That is the same sense I was making out of it. He was very career oriented. He wants to succeed in his career. Just what he said at the end, he wants money to buy the things his friends buy. It makes me wonder what is really driving him: his love for chemistry that he said he has had since high school or the money.

Shellie, Laurie, and Gwen later agreed that this attitude was a power issue, and a negative thing to have in science. In Shellie's presentation, the students were beginning to understand science as an intentional and powerful activity. With Laurie's story, they began to connect elitism with the ways that power characterized relationships in science, including their own personal relationships with each other and with science. Laurie's personal experience led the class to think through those that they had had in science that had made them feel dumb—and that feeling dumb was not always the result of intellectual inability, but rather of the elitist nature of the institution of science:

TRACY: I am glad that I did not interview him. I was intimidated to interview my person, but she turned out to be really cool, and to make me feel at ease talking with her and about her work. I think if I interviewed the person you did, Laurie, I would still feel intimidated when I left. He does not do a good job making his work accessible to people who do not like science. Like me. It seems like all he cares about is keeping his reputation, you know with the money, and talking in ways that make you feel dumb.

LAURIE: I felt dumb.

DAVE: Laurie, don't feel dumb, you understood everything he said, then shared it with us. You did a good job.

GENE: Yeah, Laurie.

GWEN: God, that guy is a jerk!

SHELLIE: No kidding!

The development of the theme of elitism was powerful in this class session because it was approached from the intersection of the two different lenses: the lens of the "other" and the lens of Western science. The lens of the other, or someone outside of the community of science, proved to be a powerful way to articulate the link between the theme of elitism and feeling dumb. Dr. Phillips held the attitude that anyone with stamina could do science and that only quality work survived the rigorous testing in place. But the students' analysis of that belief showed how that was not true. Laurie said that Dr. Phillips made her feel dumb, but I believe that our developing analysis helped her to rethink her feelings about her own intelligence and the scientific mask of elitism. Laurie's initial feelings of being dumb were not grounded solely in her experience as a woman or as a working-class person, but, rather, was an artifact of the way she has been taught to think about science and her role in science. In the conversation following Laurie's presentation on Dr. Phillips, the students created a new space from which to continue to work on their emerging ideas through disconnections between their own and Dr. Phillips's experiences. These two lenses were important because they helped the students to rethink their own experiences in science, making more visible the complex and interactive nature of their relationships with it. They helped the students articulate how they were thinking about their relationships with science.

TRACY'S ORAL HISTORY: PATTI RICKER AND
THE POLITICAL NATURE OF SCIENCE

Tracy chose to interview Patti Ricker because of Patti's background in psychology. Tracy, who worked as a secretary for a government agency, attended the college part-time in the evening to study psychology. Her goal was to transfer to the local state university and study social work. Her interest in social work shaped her actions inside and outside the classroom. When not at work, in class, or studying, she helped out at a community crisis center where she worked directly with rape and other domestic crime victims. Tracy, like Shellie and Laurie, expressed a dislike for science, and chemistry in particular, although she revealed some interest in how the brain functions and in its connections to behavior. She claimed that her real interest lay in psychology and that "psychology is not science." Earlier in the semester, she had shared that she "never thinks about science" except "little bits and pieces here and there." Tracy said that she would not have taken this course if it had not been required, and that she had not taken a science class since 10th-grade biology (which had been over 10 years ago).

Tracy's presentation occurred the week after Laurie's. Tracy shared with the class Patti Ricker's experience as a scientist, an educator, and a woman in science. The most prominent theme to emerge in Tracy's presentation was how science was inherently political, in how we are taught "our place" in science through power relationships and gender discrimination. Tracy related Patti Ricker's comments:

> She said that she became more and more uncomfortable with the traditional way of science, whether it was in the research, the questions, the experimental method. She even began to question her own ethics with her animal research. She wasn't excited about doing the research, publishing the papers, and getting the grants, like she was supposed to do. That was how success was measured. Also, she felt she wasn't taken as seriously as some of her male counterparts, as though women were less capable in this field. She felt that she was not as supported as men were in her position. . . . She said that she would change the elitist attitude that there is only one right way of doing things and that she wishes science would more seriously entertain more alternative ways about how the world works. She said that all useful research should be recognized even if it is coming from a different perspective than what we are used to. If it's legitimate research, it shouldn't be disregarded just because it is nontraditional. . . . The government spends thousands and thousands of dollars on research that isn't meaningful, and it's sometimes hard for women to get fair funding. It's sort of the old bureaucratic way.

Tracy presented the students with several provocative ideas: Patti believed science to be inequitable, particularly to women, and that science claims, unjustifiably, a position of authority in our society.

The students developed the theme of the political aspects of science by discussing the issue of power relationships. For example:

TRACY: Well, I really enjoyed talking with Patti. She was really interesting to talk to. At first I thought that I did not want to go talk to a professor and I was very nervous, but she was very personable. She turned her computer on and popped in her CD. It was nice.

SHELLIE: She sounds very interesting.

TEACHER: Why do you say that?

SHELLIE: Oh, I don't know, she reminds me of the person I interviewed. Very smart, very personable scientist. Very different image of a scientist than I usually think.

Shellie and Tracy made it evident that they felt a power relationship between themselves and science (or the scientist) where the scientist holds the more powerful position in the relationship. Yet both of these women, after conducting an oral history project on women scientists who themselves were trying to challenge the traditional social mores in the institution of science, were able to begin to critique their own ideas and experiences in science.

The financial issue of scientific research was raised. The often un-questioned assumption that money was distributed fairly within the sciences across projects and people, regardless of position, gender, or race was challenged through several students' comments. Tracy questioned who has access to money: "But I wonder who gets the money to begin with?" Laurie questioned the relationship between funding sources and science research:

> I guess I am wondering about science and technology. If you com-pare what people get money to do research for and the kinds of results they publish.

She also questioned the relationship between funding norms and "re-spect" for women in science:

> Aren't there norms? I guess it was my impression that there were norms. . . . Aren't women respected? I thought women were re-spected, at least as doctors.

In response to Laurie's concern about funding and norms, Bret voiced the implicit assumption that science is fair:

> I am sure that money is distributed fairly in science because it has to be. Isn't it regulated? There are more men in science, so it just seems like men get more money, when really that is not the case.

Finally, the ways in which our class analysis had focused on the "gender issue" was raised, as the following section of transcript indi-cates:

> SHELLIE: I find this so interesting. Since we have started these oral reports in class it seems like almost all of the women who have been interviewed with the exception of the engineer who was very positive, it seems like most of us have come back with a painted or colored picture that science is this disillusionary and that the men are the dominant force, and I am just won-

dering how the guys in here are feeling about all this stuff we
are saying.

DAVE: [Directed right at the teacher] Why do you think that it is? Is
it the men's or the women's fault? Why do you think it is?

SHELLIE: After all, this is the '90s!

As the teacher, I chose to return his question back to the class rather
than answer it myself because I felt it provided the students with an
opportunity to take their analysis a step further. The students' responses to this dilemma ranged from the defensive stance that gender
discrimination is no longer an issue because women already occupy
positions of power to the idea that things are changing. The following
three quotes represent these positions:

DAVE: There are a lot of female superintendents, level eights, and
classifieds [where I work]!

JOHN: I did not realize that things were really behind. My boss is a
female and she is head of the respiratory department. Her
right-hand person is a female. And, the boss in the branch that
I work out of is female. So, I don't know what I think.

GWEN: I think it is changing but it has been a recent change. I have
a sister, for example, who is 4 years older and she was a senior
in high school and had a final in physics and it was a curved
grade and she tied with a male. He received an A and she received a B, because quote unquote, it is more important for a
boy to do well in school. . . . This was 20 years ago and there
can only be so much changing that can be evolved because if
you think about how we get our ideas of how we socialize together as men and women, a lot of them from our parents.
Twenty years ago is a generation. All right, now a lot of the
parents from that time, that raised that particular person and
that mentality of the time, they are still grandparents and it's
not that far enough evolved to be a big enough change. . . . So
I think that with time it will get better, but I don't think there
is a blame or a fault. It's just socialization and how it is evolving.

The conversation following Tracy's oral history on Patti Ricker
pushed the class's thinking on the political nature of science and, in
particular, how this shapes funding in science and the experiences of
women. Tracy's emphasis on Patti's experience as a woman in science
and the discrimination endemic to her practice in science forced the

members of the class to rethink the disillusionment with science that we had talked about in connection to the human element and elitism. As the previous section of transcript indicates, the students began to rethink some of the things they never really thought to question, such as the number of women in the workplace or their experiences in school.

The messages about science and who can do science were intensified in Tracy's report when several of the students began to draw connections across oral histories. Just as Shellie had discussed Lisa's disillusionment with science and the elitist attitude that Lisa had confronted, so Tracy described Patti's dilemmas. These two oral history projects created a space in which students such as Gwen, John, and Shellie could seriously reconsider their experiences in what they now saw as a highly politicized science. When the oral history conversations were defined by students' making connections between personal experiences and humanness, elitism, and politics, it became difficult to view science as an objective, detached, impersonal, and unemotional endeavor. A more complex picture of science emerged when students linked the analysis spawned by Tracy's report to the previous oral history conversations and their personal experiences and feelings.

GENE'S ORAL HISTORY: KAREN ROSS AND WEAVING THE THEMES TOGETHER

Gene, in his late 50s and a former player in the National Football League, was studying chemistry to become a certified physical science teacher. Although not new to education—he had been a physical education teacher for nearly 20 years—he was new to science teaching. He was in his 1st year of teaching physical science to urban ninth graders. Gene's oral history project was on Karen Ross, a science education professional.

Unlike many of the students in this course, Gene "like[d] science at its core." He liked "to observe" and "to figure things out." He liked "to think through situations," "to use his intellect," and "not just to do something because he was told." He wanted his own science students at the high school to develop those same qualities.

Gene introduced his oral history report by offering a biographical sketch of Karen Ross. He told us that Karen first became interested in science when she was young through "the outdoors stuff" and through the influence of a "chemistry family." She had explored science as a high school and college student not because of particular employment opportunities, but because of the many options that it provided. With a science background, Karen could pursue a career in forestry or in marine biology as well as think more deeply about the kinds of things that made her wonder, such as the "complex and intriguing chemistry in a leaf."

Gene described how Karen used science in her profession. This piece of his presentation opened up a complex web of ideas about elitism in science, the political nature of science, and the need for a human element in science and about how important these ideas were for science teachers to consider. He concluded by sharing how Karen had experienced discrimination in science merely because of her gender and in science education because of her "female" perspective. As Gene told the class,

> [Karen] felt that her views were too feminine about the connection with nature and the natural connection between science, chemistry, and nature and so forth which was something that apparently wasn't masculine enough for her peers. . . . She also said that science perpetuates that by saying you aren't smart enough and that the science department is also saying to people you aren't smart enough, we don't want you. How can you ignore all these things about science when they are real? If you feel like you understand pretty good, and then they tell you that, then you, you can't.

Gene's comment went right to my heart. I struggled with ways to make the class more liberating so that students would not feel oppressed by science. His comment suggested to me that after so many years of schooling and of participating in society, he understood that the elitist practices in science had not changed. He understood that unless he participated on their terms and met the expectations set through these practices, he would still be considered a failure in the eyes of science. I felt a bittersweet hopefulness knowing that Gene had used some of the critiques of science to make sense of his own "failed participation" in it.

Yet I could not lose this opportunity to pursue Gene's comment. I believed (and as I felt that Gene was beginning to argue) that the practices of the institution of science and science education can serve to perpetuate the elitist status of science through the ways in which it chooses to determine who can or cannot do science. So I told the class that "I feel that way with this course and the way that they have designed it. They try to make it so that many students do poorly or fail. You have to have an average exam score of 70%, you have to make sure you have a 30% fail or drop rate. You have to have five exams and you have to cover 17 chapters in 15 weeks. Who cares if you understand the material or can find ways to use it or make sense of it in your lives?'' Gene immediately responded to my comment:

> I think that's traditional in science classes. Thinking back to my freshman year at [university], we had a freshman science class, and there were about a thousand people in the lecture hall, and the prof, I remember he looked at us and said, on the 1st day, look to your right and look to your left, you won't see these people come next semester. Over half of you won't make it to the second semester because you'll drop or your grades won't make it.

Gene's comment about his own science education was all too similar to what is advocated by the chemistry department at Ashton. Although the department seemed outwardly and even genuinely concerned with helping as many people through science as possible, there also seemed to be this unspoken glory in the fact that our introductory chemistry course was known around Ashton as ''the hardest course on campus,'' and that over one third of the students dropped the course before midsemester. Gwen brought Gene's message back to Ashton:

> I had [a different prof] last semester and I dropped the course and let me tell you why. When I got my first exam back, I got a 60% and he suggested that I drop the course unless I wanted to be in for a big struggle for the rest of the semester. So I listened to him and I dropped the course. Now I wonder why did I drop the course because it wasn't like I did anything between now and then to get more ready, and here I am taking the course again, and I am doing fine. But he told me to drop the course.

Gwen's comment about her experiences at Ashton led the students to question the chemistry program at the college: its status as the hardest course on campus, its high drop-out and failure rate, and the role of the teachers in the program. For example, the students' questions led us to calculate together the total percentage of people who actually passed the course in any given semester (based on some data that I had about retention and failure rates in the course). I started out by assembling the data:

> Let me see, do I have those statistics with me? I only have the statistics for [Introductory Chemistry] because that is the only course I teach. Let's see, here it is. Last year, across all the sections

there was a 46% drop rate. . . . Let's say we had 100 people lined up. Forty-six dropped the course, 54 are left. Out of these people who are left, guess how many failed the course. . . . Twenty-nine%. That's almost a third of the people who are left; let's see, a third of 54 is nearly 17 more people. That means that out of the 100 people who started the course, 100 minus 46 minus 17 is about 37. Thirty-seven people pass. That's only a little bit more than two thirds, no wait, one third of the people who sign up for the course make it to the end with a passing grade. My question is, how can they justify that?

This exercise raised even more questions about the different forces at play keeping students out of science. Sue and Shellie questioned the role of the teacher:

SUE: What about the other teachers? Couldn't they realize if you were doing that bad, that it might not always be the student?
SHELLIE: I had another chemistry teacher tell me that if you have a three point on your first test, you better get out.

Kristin and Laurie questioned the role of Ashton as an institution:

KRISTIN: Do you think [Ashton] do[es] it to get the money?
LAURIE: They make a lot of money. If you think about it, they make a lot of money. They are doing it for financial reasons.
TEACHER: I never thought about that, I just know that when I found out, I could hardly believe it and I am really embarrassed by it.

Finally, Shellie questioned my own role within the organizational structures that appeared at this point to promote student failure:

Do you find yourself getting discouraged when you bump up against that regularly? Or do you get more motivated to make some changes?

The conversation following Gene's report marked what I consider to be a second turning point for our class because we used our developing critiques to begin to rewrite our science education. Throughout the conversation, we continued to build a critique of our experiences in science through the themes of elitism, the human element, and the political nature of science. With each new oral history conversation, the same set of contradictory ideas about science emerged. They reinforced the notion that neither our lives, nor the lives of the people represented through the oral histories, were isolated cases and provided growing support for more and more students to talk out about their own less-than-satisfactory experiences in science. It was not that our experiences were identical. Quite the contrary. It was more that there was an evasive yet nevertheless present set of power arrangements active in our science experiences that generated an equally evasive yet present set of arti-facts—elitism and ahumanism. Gwen, for example, shared her experi-ences in the introductory chemistry class that she had dropped a semes-ter earlier because the professor did not want (have time? believe it was not important?) to consider the needs of the students. Gene talked about the "elitist" attitude of a science teacher he had had in college several years earlier. Shellie expressed frustration about the "weeding-out" process in science and wondered why everyone who so desired could not be a scientist.

We then used our developing critique to begin to deconstruct our own situations at Ashton and to begin to build our own science educa-tion. Before this class session, the students had not been aware of the high drop rate for the course. What they did know about the course was mainly learned through hearsay: It was supposed to be the toughest course on campus and if you could not score at least a 3.0 on the first quiz then you were doomed to fail. We spoke about the practices in the chemistry department that made some of us feel inadequate as students and as teachers. This process of deconstructing the practices in the de-partment began another in which we began to rewrite our own science education.

REPOSITIONING CHEMISTRY THROUGH ORAL HISTORIES

Through the oral history projects and related science class discussions, the students and I created spaces of radical resistance that informed our efforts to rethink science. Central to this process was making explicit our own identities and experiences in science. Through conversations surrounding the projects, we had a context in which to reveal aspects of ourselves—who we were as learners of science, as gendered, raced, and classed people—that we might not have been able to have in the context of regular school science. The students and I were able to construct spaces in which to make public our nontraditional science ideas. This is important because in mainstream science education, the focus of classroom discourse in on "key concepts and principles." Normally, when experience is brought into science class, it is channeled into defending and validating a particular kind of science. Allowing lived experiences to bring to the forefront the positional nature of the knower and knowing in science denies the possibility in an objective reality. It opens up science and science learning to cacophony. It allows teachers and students to experience how knowledge about science and in science embodies the complex and contradictory locations of the lives of those who construct that knowledge. The creation of these spaces pushed against the boundaries of Western science and as a result, as a community, we were able to begin to decenter the traditional power arrangements in science. We were able to reposition ourselves in science. In what follows, I explore the power of the oral histories in our efforts to create spaces of radical resistance.

The oral histories, much more than official subject matter knowledge, served as a source of critical repositioning of science in our class. One reason for their power was that they were not bounded, unlike exploration of subject matter. When we talked about states of matter, for example, there was the unwritten and unspoken rule that despite anything else the students and I might have done (such as critiques or revisioning), the students would eventually be responsible for "knowing the canon." With the oral histories, we had more freedom to explore issues that connected with personal needs and experiences. When we talked about the experiences of Patti Ricker, Lisa Karms, or Karen Ross, there was no set expectation for what we would cover. There was no department chair and no textbook telling us what we had to say and what we had to learn to be considered knowledgeable in those particular areas. There was a freedom to talk about the lives of these people in ways that meant something to us because they connected with our experiences in and out of science and not because they connected with the textbook or the department curriculum.

Another reason for the power of the oral histories was that they enabled us to create spaces of radical resistance that informed our efforts to reposition science. They allowed us to share our own identities and experiences in science rather than remain "voiceless," as many students felt was expected in the sciences. Through our conversations, we created a context in which to reveal aspects of ourselves, which we might not have been able to do in the context of science. Sharon Welch (1985) writes that "the disclosure of suppressed systems is part of an insurrection of the subjugated knowledges" (p. 74). I believe that the oral histories created a space for the disclosure of the complexity of our lives, which is delegitimized by science. Our connection to the oral histories through our valuing our own life histories allowed us to begin to critique the subjugating knowledges of science.

Laurie, Gene, and John connected with Lisa Karms's disillusionment, caused by the lack of the human element in science. Through articulating experiences of when in their own lives they had encountered a need for the human element in science, each in her or his own way was able to partially uncover how the institutions of science and education work to suppress this. On another occasion, the students, led by Gene, Gwen, and Laurie, taught me to see how the department works in tandem with the science community to perpetuate elitism in science. Through their courage and their own political resistance, they helped me to act on my own developing beliefs.

Finally, the oral histories gave the students a language to reread their experiences in and out of science. In this process of rearticulating experiences, the students were able to reposition their relationships with science. The students' ongoing critique of the human element made science without an explicit human connection unacceptable in our class. The students began to define their own science and their own relationship with that science. In the conversations about the various oral history projects that I have discussed here, we had the chance to problematize what is acceptable in science by valuing our contradictory lived experiences. Discussing the lives of women and men who have been disillusioned and unfairly treated as well as successful in science helped us to rethink and rewrite our own experiences in science. Furthermore, as the oral histories progressed across the semester, so did the complexity and subtlety of the critiques emerging from our conversations, which worked their way into our study of chemistry. As the conversations became more complex, the interactions between the oral histories and our learning of chemistry became more complex. This was particularly the case toward the end of the semester, when we collectively decided to engage in "acts of political resistance" by throwing out the department's requirements for the course and rewriting our own, recognizing that this might cost me my job.

Welch writes that moments of resistance are "an affirmation of an identity that is different from that imposed by the dominant patriarchal social structures . . . a declaration of the possibility of freedom and justice" (p. 42). Our "moments of resistance" in science class shifted our relationships within the power structure arranged by the dominant patriarchal social framework of science and education, because we experienced ourselves and our ideas about science differently. We formed our own creative community of resistance. Although I had begun the semester hoping to work through the oppression that many women studying science experience as a result of the domineering patriarchal structure of science, I learned by listening to my students that this patriarchal aspect is inextricably bound up in a capitalist agenda. I believe that this helped us all dig into our experiences to find memories of oppression in science. Understanding and critiquing our own and each other's stories helped build solidarity.

I have learned through watching the students make connections between theoretical critiques of science and their experiences with science that central to any revisioned science is providing students with opportunities to deconstruct the mythical images of science and scientists and revealing how our visions of science are produced within relations of power and social, cultural, and historical practices. Creating contexts in which the science education regime of objectivity, homogeneity, and universal validity are interrogated contextually by students and teacher—interrogated through our cultural and gender-specific experiences—makes problematic pedagogical and scientific practices that inform and legitimate hegemonic visions of reality. A revisioned science requires a space and a language in which to make public our nontraditional science ideas so we may begin to decenter the traditional power relationships in science and education.

The oral history conversations gave us a language and a space in which to resist and refuse alienating practices of science that we had experienced through the promotion of science as nonsubjective—removed from personal, social, political, and historical experiences in our lives or in the lives of others. The oral histories helped us to think critically about our lives as science teachers and learners, men and women, by insisting that we make "explicit our historical and social place as a concretely lived reality that touches us, like the wind, imperceptibly and yet unmistakably" (Lewis, 1993, p. 54). I believe, in the words of bell hooks (1994), that they helped us to "decolonize" our science minds.

4

Learning About Ourselves Inside of Science, Outside of Science

In the middle of April, Tracy missed one week of class to attend a counselor training session for a domestic violence and sexual assault hotline. When she came back to class, she wrote in her journal:

> A break from Listening Ear Training! While this is a worthwhile experience and will come in handy often, I'm concerned about my chem and social work. It seems like it's always one or the other. Only one more week!

In response, I wrote in Tracy's journal:

> I think your presentation on Patti was exciting. It stimulated a great discussion. How did hearing Patti talk about her experiences in and beliefs about chemistry make you feel as a woman studying science? I am also curious, because of your last entry, if you see any connection at all between what you want to do with counseling and chemistry.

To this Tracy replied in her journal a week later:

> Angie, to answer your question, I am not sure how chemistry is going to relate to my desired profession. It may be useful in the sense of the neurosciences, as Patti Ricker had mentioned, or possibly in the use of different medications and their effect on the body or the psyche. I have not yet taken cognitive psyche, but I am sure that my chemistry will have some impact on my career-to-be. Thanks for your asking! Your question made me put into words my expectations of chemistry use.
>
> Needless to say, I was quite disappointed in myself after the

last test. While I missed the coverage of chapter 14, I felt like I had an understanding of chapters 12 and 13. The only explanation I can think of for my open-book, open-notes test would be just being completely emotionally and physically drained. Even though my classes and studies have suffered over the last 2 weeks, I must say that I have learned some very valuable skills and have personally grown through the listening and ear training. I don't think there ever would be a good time to do it. I highly recommend it if you are even the least bit interested.

Maybe we could do lunch sometime after the semester is over with? It would be interesting to hear more of your experiences with education and feminism. I guess this is enough writing for now. Thanks for your concern this evening. Time to study.

By now, it was the end of the semester and so as my last response to Tracy in her journal, I replied:

I enjoyed having you as a student in this course. Good luck in psychology. [One] of the things that I have tried to do in this course (although not always explicitly) was to bring a feminist perspective to teaching science by (1) with the class, deconstructing notions of elitism in science, (2) refusing to uncritically accept the authority of Ashton to tell us what to teach and learn, (3) making explicit the culture of power and relationships of power and privilege in science (i.e., domination by the old boy network by controlling research money and the decision of what is acceptable scientific behavior and research subjects), (4) heightening awareness, and (5) allowing the voices of women scientists to be heard—including the students in the class and the oral histories (if you notice, my list for oral histories is 90% women. I wanted their voices to be heard, for they are rarely heard in the science community). I think with some of these issues I was more successful than others. Mostly I think in meeting my feminist goals, I failed. I feel that as a feminist teacher of science, I am silenced by the requirements of a department that does not understand the sexist domination in the sciences and by a general attitude about science and science education in a society that does not value the experiences of women. Well, there is always next semester.

Since my dissertation is closely related to what I just wrote, I am curious to get feedback from students. Do you think that this course in any way (in any little way) contributed to breaking away from the status quo and from maintaining oppressive relationships in the sciences?

I know that psychology is equally dominated by men and male worldviews. I hope that you can hang in there and begin to create change in the way that psychology is practiced. Following is a list of readings that you might find interesting. (You might have read some that are already on the list). Let's have lunch.

The conversations that Tracy and I shared throughout the semester in her journal served as a starting point for the various conversations that I had with spring semester students during the summer semester following our course together. Her initial invitation for me to join her at lunch provided my first realization of the value of conversation about chemistry and of critiques of chemistry outside the formal classroom structures. Throughout the semester, I tried to engage students in conversation, believing that we could overlook the power imbalance inherent in our relationship, to engage in meaningful, sincere conversation about our feelings and experiences in science. Although I think some of our in-class conversations were intense, and no matter how much I hoped that we could overcome the power imbalance, our in-class relationship was nonetheless bounded and limited by our inscribed identities within the classroom. How much could the students really risk sharing with me, the one who ultimately would decide their academic fates in the class, the one who served as the link to the larger institution?

Tracy's invitation to lunch served as invitation for me to question how my own embeddedness in the educational and science institutions and how my sometimes passive acceptance of these boundaries constrained my interpretations of what it means to teach and learn chemistry. Tracy's intervention enabled me to ask myself for the first time, why bind my teaching role to traditional structures? Aren't these the structures that I am seeking to change? Why does all my "teaching" work have to be done in the classroom where my attempts to deconstruct the teacher-student relationship remain bound up in the hierarchical relationships of education and science? Why not take teaching and learning into new contexts where we can explore issues uninhibited by our institutions? I was not sure what to expect from the summer conversations, and I was a bit nervous having to construct a new kind of relationship with these students.

In this chapter, I explore a series of summer conversations that I shared with a small group of students from the spring semester (Tracy, Laurie, and Gene). I describe how the act of engaging in these conversations simultaneously pushed against the prescribed boundaries of science education and made these boundaries visible for the students and for me. This is important because, as I argued earlier, one of the reasons that I wanted to keep positionality as a central theme in my teacher research was to help me articulate the ways in which physical and intellectual structures inscribe identities in the teaching, learning, and doing of science. Through stories and conversation about school, science, families, and personal lives, Gene, Tracy, and Laurie shed some light on three themes that I believe characterize feminist science teaching: critical awareness, praxis, and moving relationships. Here, I weave meaning through these themes by bringing to the center the voices of Gene, Tracy, and Laurie and my reflections on what it is that I believe they are telling the science education community. After each theme is discussed separately, they are brought together to complexify, challenge, deconstruct, and complicate my definition of feminist science teaching and the role positionality plays in such an endeavor.

CRITICAL AWARENESS

[When I think about scientific knowledge,] I think about what does it mean to mix things and what do you have to know. What goes into a cappuccino or a French soda? The gasoline. I think about it a lot more. I am more conscious of something being a part of science, going over the everyday types of substances—solids, gases, and liquids, that sort of thing. . . . it makes me more mad that they don't give me more options. One thing is very evident, at least in the book that we used: very rarely is a woman's name mentioned, and I think that I have become more aware of this. Women are practically nonexistent. You know that is not the way that happened unless they were jailed or burned at the stake. So I guess I would like to make it more broad. Give you more options as to what you want to believe and why. Encourage the student to make their own decisions. (Tracy, Conversation in coffee shop, June 15, 1994)

GENE: I think the elitist attitude makes me feel angry at the injustice that attitude emulates to the everyday spectator in regards to any type of knowledge, teaching, concept, philosophy; and it holds, it bestows, a false sense of superiority that the professor, elitist, has. The anger I feel is that the student or the masses will have to feel insubordinate or they can't have an opportunity to attain the knowledge. It made me feel good to know some real interesting things about science.

TEACHER: This is very interesting. Do you think before the chemistry class last semester you would have said the same thing?

GENE: I do not think that I would have said the elitism. Well no, not all of them, either.

TEACHER: What do you mean by that? Or let me say that in the best and worst worlds what do you mean?

GENE: Let me give an example. The worst situation is where the scientist sits back in the ivory tower and works on solving problems in the physical world.

TEACHER: Why is this a worst case?

GENE: Because they are sitting back up in their ivory towers and this is elitist because they are just sitting up there, with no care or connection to the masses. Who cares about the masses? But the best situation is where the scientist goes out actively and joins the masses and is able to relate to the everyday person who is trying to find answers. They need to be more human. They need to be out and about and stimulate educational growth. Contact with the common man, the common person, is important. Like in manufacturing they get into the nitty-gritty, they have to make it work. They are playing the science game, and making things useful for the future. At the college level, it can be just like teaching. In the science methods course, they never covered the stuff that I need on the front line. Anybody can talk about subject matter knowledge. But I learned more about science in my 1st year of teaching than I did in 4 years of college. (In local restaurant, June 15, 1994)

LAURIE: I think that taking chemistry helped me to understand the psychology of why some people go into science. It made me think about scientists and where they come from. Most interestingly, on TV recently there was an interview with some doctors in Russia. Did you see that one, it was on 60 Minutes?

TEACHER: No.

LAURIE: Doctors in Russia don't get paid as much as the bus drivers. It was just, a lot of it, the scientists, the values that they place in society on their field. The value system of Russia versus the U.S. It made me wonder what caused that, the value system difference. It makes me wonder about the value system and the difference.

TEACHER: What do you think caused that difference? Well, first, what do you think that the value system of science in the U.S. is based on?

LAURIE: Values of science in the United States are economics. Economics are the value system. Oh, and science holds the answers, especially in the medical field. Medicine in the field, you know dominance in your life. Some, I guess that some, I think part of it is that accessibility to medical treatment is much more dominant in the U.S. versus Russia. What's present in everyday life—what you get used to having as your standard of living. So, I think maybe it boils down to the standard of living you are having. (Over cookies in my office, June 14, 1994)

As bell hooks (1994) wrote, "It is not easy to name our pain, to theorize from that location" (p. 74). Developing a critical awareness in our lives *of* our lives is not an easy thing to do. It is also not without pain or struggle. But by developing a critical awareness of ourselves and of the science in our lives that has, through sexist, racist, and capitalist intentions, dominated and dissected us, I believe that we can begin to rename the power structures that define us in science. But what does it mean for students to develop a critical awareness of science and of themselves as users and producers of science? What are the tensions and contradictions inherent in this process?

The stories, ideas, and experiences that Tracy, Laurie, and Gene share bring out two important aspects of the theme of critical awareness: awareness and understanding of scientific concepts and the ways in which they influence personal and societal life, and awareness and understanding of the things about science that cause feelings of alienation and marginalization. Having an awareness and an understanding of scientific concepts and the ways in which they influence personal life was important because it was practical and interesting. For example, Tracy talked about being able to use her scientific understandings in her everyday life, from questioning what goes into a French soda to making decisions about gasoline. Gene talked about making dietary decisions, about whether to drink chlorinated water:

We drink chlorinated water, right. Part of the ignorance is that we just accept the fact that we drink chlorinated water. What do we even know, as everyday people, what that does? What if chlorinated water is not even good for you? All these toxins can be captured by your body. We are taught to accept that it is okay because it does something good. But, what else does it do?

Having an awareness and understanding of the things about science that cause feelings of alienation and marginalization dominated more of the summer conversation time. For example, three of the biggest themes for Tracy, Laurie, and Gene appeared to be the "elitist" attitude in science, the control of science and, in particular, medicine by economic forces, and the lack of a role for science in their lives. Laurie talked about the psychology of why people go into science and the values they espouse. Gene talked about the discrimination against women in science and "that it doesn't have to be that way." He also talked about how little the scientific community tells the general public and how that effects the amount that the general public knows or believes they need to know: "There is ignorance and intelligence. No matter how smart, there is ignorance."

Gene struggled with the elitism theme in ways that were very telling. He wanted science to be more subjective so that we could make a connection to the "masses." He brought up the injustices done to women in the past that will end in the future. Finally, he talked about the coexistence of intelligence and ignorance among the masses. I wondered why Gene chose the word *masses*. Did he see large groups of us— like his students—not having access to science and being herded around by the scientists because they are ignorant of the ways in which the scientific community controls them? Was his own need to make science more subjective a way to get science into the masses so that they cannot be herded? Did he think that this subjectivity in science will stop the discrimination against women and girls, or did he think that finding ways to bring the masses in will actually change science so that it is more friendly to these groups?

Developing a critical awareness of science and self-in-science is not without its own tensions. There certainly was a tension that existed between learning science and critiquing science brought on by critical awareness. Yet Laurie, Tracy, and Gene found ways to coexist in the two worlds of learning and critiquing science; they went on with their complex lives, creating meaning from their own multiple and contradictory positionings. As Tracy pointed out, the tension between these competing agendas is useful—if not necessary—in science class. This is because it is our articulation, our own recognition of what we understand and how we understand it. It is the articulation of this tension that allow us to remain critical because it helps to make explicit how we position ourselves in learning and doing science.

PRAXIS

GENE: I think that I learned a lot from talking and from talking about my and your frustrations about how important it is for science to be more human. I saw you struggle with that, about you trying to make it that way. That is very admirable. That's a sign of things to come. You have touched on something that has got to happen. We have got to be a more enlightened society. It's got to happen. It's got to be more human. We have to strive to make a connection with the masses. We need to start at school, at home, with parents. It's got to happen. (In coffee shop, June 22, 1994)

GENE: We have to change science. Only at that level, at the teaching level, not only as a member of society. . . . The injustices performed to females [by] science would [be] in past and present but not the future. And that it doesn't have to be that way. There is ignorance and intelligence. No matter how smart, there is ignorance. It comes from the church: Woman is submissive and man is dominant. This is based on the ignorant male in society. It makes me feel like I can be different and don't have to be a part of that message. We have choices. For me to feel good, I don't need to make someone else feel bad. I would say that at least 60% of the kids in [my] school, do not get the right nutrition. We got so many processed foods. There are so many things in science related to improving the quality of life. Putting processed foods has pickled the American people.

TEACHER: That kind of grosses me out.

GENE: Well, they did studies over in Vietnam. If an American got shot, if a Vietnamese got killed on the battlefield, it took them 12 hours before the body started to decompose. If an American got killed on the battlefield, it took 46 hours to start to decompose. They were actually pickled with something like monosodium glutamate. They were pickled, and that is because of all of the processed foods that we eat. . . . There is so much power there. There is a lot of ignorance, that science lives on. (pause) We drink chlorinated water, right. Part of the ignorance is that we just accept the fact that we drink chlorinated water. What do we even know, as everyday people, what that does? What if chlorinated water is not even good for you? All these toxins can be captured by your body. We are taught to accept that it is okay because it does something good. But, what else does it do? (In coffee shop, June 29, 1994)

Praxis, or reflection action, is a theme integrally related to critical awareness, for as the summer conversations highlight, praxis is using critical awareness to act upon the world to change things, and an understanding that each individual can alone, and as a collective, actively shape that process. As Gene explained, this process requires a recognition of human agency. In other words, part of feminist praxis in science class is finding ways to help all students use their agentic positions to challenge ideas, beliefs, and relations in science that silence or oppress lived experiences. Gene, an urban high school teacher, discussed how "science does not care about the masses," and that we need to find ways to engage the masses in science so that they too will be enlightened. Gene challenged the authority of science through his life as high school physical science teacher, not necessarily from feelings of alienation. On several occasions, he expressed how much he likes science "at its core." But at the high school, he had a boss who told him how and what to teach, despite the fact that this boss had no formal training in the sciences. When Gene realized, furthermore, that the current situation at school did not make his own agency possible, he talked about how he needed to act on that to do what he felt was right. In one of the summer conversations, he disclosed that he was leaving his current job at the local high school to take on a new job teaching science and coaching football in a town nearly 100 miles away. He referred to all the talk in our class about elitism and said that he experienced a similar sort of thing at his high school. He said that he was "sick of being on the bottom" of those sorts of relationships. He was sick of not being listened to by his local and district administrators. He was sick of not having his teaching ideas valued. He felt that he was not growing, and nor were his students, because of the circumstances. Most of all, he was sick of the political nature of school and of science and how everyone seemed to deny the politics. He seemed really excited about moving because he felt would be at a place where he could enact his agenda of reaching the masses.

Praxis is, by its nature, evolving. I did not need to know a revisioned science to teach to the students, in order for us to do feminist praxis. Rather, feminist praxis existed through creating opportunities in science class to understand how knowledge was constructed through experiences, how such knowledge reflected subjectivities, and how it related to power, privilege, and oppression. By creating opportunities in science class for critical exploration of lived experiences—as we did with the oral histories, and most certainly did through our summer conversations—we were able to reconstruct scientific knowledge that did not deny or oppress our lived experiences, and required us to rethink agency in the sciences.

Praxis is also political. Gene's ideas about who gets to know what in science and society point to the fact that part of a feminist agenda are the political intentions that shape and guide the efforts to help students become aware of the power relationships in science and how these relationships shape their definitions of science, scientific knowledge, and the self-in-science. This is political because the underlying goal of helping students to understand these relationships is helping them change them as well. It is important to deconstruct with students the teacher-student dichotomy, and that of the scientist-nonscientist. As Gene asked, "How much of our lives do we not even question just because we do not even know enough to realize that there is a question to be asked?" I wonder how much of our lives in and out of chemistry class we have passively accepted or silenced because our roles have unknowingly been defined for us. In chemistry class, as teachers and students, we defined ourselves in our relationship with each other, the educational process, and science (and in turn were also being defined by these structures). We learned to construct meaning within these relationships. Yet because of the ideological underpinnings of science education, we learned to think about science and ourselves through the boundaries of inscribed dichotomies, even when these did not speak to our experiences or understandings of the world. As Davies (1989) writes, engaging in socially defined dualisms means "being socially competent" or "not being deviant." Thus, teaching is inherently political in its facilitating—and often validating—particular power arrangements and the associated knowledges. The whole idea of feminist liberatory science education as praxis is a strong argument that simply presenting students with a critique of science is not enough to challenge these relationships. This is exactly what Gene illustrated when he examined his personal situation at his high school and learned more about his diet. Consequently, he changed his job and his diet. We need to find aspects of our lives where these critiques play out in order to begin to rewrite our lives and our relationships with science.

Feminist praxis as a basis for science education rests on our ability to construct new kinds of relationships in science that allow for the expression of the full range of our lived experiences. Feminist praxis as a basis for science education also helps us to view these relationships as political and evolving and as situated by our positionality. This framework makes it possible to change those relationships so that they reflect and embody inclusive visions of self and science.

MOVING RELATIONSHIPS

TEACHER: I know that a lot of the issues that I want to raise can be
    so personal, really connect with you at a personal level and to
    ask people to do that in a public setting with people who they
    are not friends with is difficult. I think it gets easier as the se-
    mester continues because you build some sort of community,
    at least I hope, and think we have built some sort of commu-
    nity, but still, we are very much strangers. I know that some-
    times I said a lot about myself and then afterwards I wondered
    why I said so much.

TRACY: Sometimes when you revealed more of yourself, it helped
    me to think about and say some things about myself. It's that
    trust thing: If you open up, then maybe everyone else will
    open up. (In coffee shop, June 29, 1994)

LAURIE: How powerful the field of science is and how controlling.
    How it has a strong dominance in the economy in a lot of
    ways. I mean, how our government has safeguards to make
    sure that we are protected against things like chemicals, and
    the new discoveries and how long it takes a drug to be ap-
    proved. I don't think that there are enough checks and bal-
    ances. It's a positive for the economy, it's positive for the sci-
    ences if stuff goes out in the economy and not if it is held back.

TEACHER: Tell me more about the government thing. How does
    this last thing make you feel as a person, as a woman in our so-
    ciety?

LAURIE: This makes me crazy because there are so many things,
    there are so many chemicals, and there are probably drugs out
    there that might benefit people but there are so many, you
    know, political, or even values, that prevent them from not be-
    ing passed. You know they would help certain people, so that
    I am sure that there are many chemicals out there that are caus-
    ing cancer. Cancer is just too prevalent. There is not enough
    emphasis on studying. One of my friends is going into medical
    geography and that is fascinating.

TEACHER: Oh neat, what is that?

LAURIE: They study trends of different diseases and things like that
    that are occurring; high cancer rates in this region or high
    [rates of] this type of disease, like medical disease types of
    trends.

TEACHER: Wow, I just learned in the Midwest there are a large num-
    ber of people, of babies being born with holes in their hearts.

Much more than the national average. I only learned about this last summer, because my sister who lives in Cincinnati, her daughter was born with a hole in her heart.

LAURIE: I have heard of that. But I mean I think that the scientists hold back so much information from the public. Then the media chips away, and then you never really find out the truth because of government controls. It is such a controlling factor in your life and you don't have access to it. I think you have a right to that. That is what bothers me the most when it comes to those chemicals that are killing you. You never know until it is too late or so many people have died. It's just, science controls every aspect of our lives. You don't have, you are not given, the rights you should have. Science controls all that information, so does the government. . . . I have thought about it before because I am from a small town and there are so many people who are dying of cancer and you know it's got to be from the fertilizer. . . . I am from Ashford. My mother had a really good friend that died of cancer just in the village and almost everyone had died of cancer. There are just too many. There are a lot of people out there with cancer. Just a small farming community. To see all the people with cancer in such a small geographic area. I mean there is just so much cancer around, in the small towns, that just bothers me. I can't believe that they haven't figured out that there is a problem or what is causing it. It is so obvious that all these people are getting cancer. Why can't they figure it out? I think they know some of the things and they just don't want to let it out because it is going to have a drastic effect on the economy. Why don't they really know? They know so many other things, like with what NASA can do and I mean I think that the technology is there. Maybe it's not, you just don't know. I guess that is why, well I can understand too it's a complicated area. They are coming out more and more with genetic findings and they have to be really close, and they might know it already and not want to say or help. Just like with the [inaudible] and all that, I can't believe that it's happening, there is living proof that it causes problems, but they are really not doing much. They haven't taken it off the market, but they haven't done anything about it. (Over cookies in my office, June 14, 1994)

A third theme that characterizes feminist science teaching and that was brought out in the summer conversations is moving relationships. I use the phrase *moving relationships*[1] to imply several ideas. First, I use the term to suggest that relationships are contextually dependent. The relationships we have in class with each other and with science are in constant change because how we view knowledge and how we view ourselves is contextually dependent (Haraway, 1988). Relationships are negotiated intersubjectively through power arrangements and are dependent upon the backgrounds that the participants bring to such interactions (Rommetveit, 1980). Tracy's talk about sharing personal experience and trust illustrates that relationships in science class are determined publicly and socially through our collective set of lived experiences, rather than by the private intention of either the students or the teacher. Our relationships with each other and with science shift as we encounter new situations, new ideas, and new people. As Gergen (1991) writes, "The trajectory of coordinated efforts of any two persons will thus be vitally influenced by these multiple enmeshments. As any two develop as a relational unit, we are the common interstice or point of confrontation for a multiple of relationships" (p. 586). Here, Gergen is advocating that we are defined by our relationships, that we are involved in a "multiplicity of relational processes" (p. 585), and that these relationships move as we engage in new experiences and encounter new people.

Laurie created for herself a critique of science that was firmly grounded in her lived experiences. This is important: "We, as students and teachers, come to know and understand through the filters of our experiences, our social positions in life and work and our senses of personal (and political) agency" (Hollingsworth, 1994a, p. 1). Before this conversation with Laurie, I had known that it was possible for us to reread our experiences with and in science in ways that did not silence, oppress, or diminish them—we had begun to do that through our oral history conversations and through our critique of the department. I had known that these rereadings and rearticulations of our lives in and out of science were the source of our ability to construct new relationships with it. Yet conversations with Laurie, Tracy, and Gene highlight how a feminist science can not be developed by me (or anyone else) until we come to class with some essentialized notion of what it means to be a woman or a member of a minority group. It is dependent on our ability to reread the nature of science from our multiple standpoints.

Second, the relationships are moving in that they are affective; they reflect and embody passion. This notion highlights the feminist position that the relationships that we have in science class incorporate much more than just subject matter knowledge. Learning a feminist science implies creating a science education that brings in the whole being, not just the intellect as posited through the positivist notion of the mind/body split, and not just the subject matter knowledge in both content and process as suggested through many state and national reform initiatives. Bringing in the whole being means exploring ourselves in science—not just examining our knowledge. Laurie's interrogation of the cancer rates in her town is an example of how relationships with science involve the whole being physically, mentally, and emotionally. For Laurie to examine these cancer trends and causes, she had to accept how they affected her own life. Our conversation about her predicament captures the ways in which our relationships with science change when we create opportunities to reread our lived experiences. She questioned what she had observed and reflected on where she could obtain more information.

Laurie began the semester with a "negative attitude" about science. Learning more about her family history, the rate of cancer in her area, the lack of knowledge dissemination about cancer in her community, and the detached stance of the government and the science community toward the epidemic speaks very clearly to me that no amount of "fun, hands-on activities," cooperative groups, or positive role models in science would have made science a positive experience for Laurie. Her community was disproportionately affected by cancer and no one (as far as she can tell—her reality was a valid one) was intervening to improve the situation through education or regulations. This suggests to me that a feminist science is much more than "female-friendly" classroom practices. It is highly and intensely political and requires an interrogation of science from marginalized lived experiences.

Furthermore, Tracy's understanding of what it means to be a female nonscientist gave her a chance to work through and change definitions of herself imposed on her in science education. At the beginning of the semester, she believed that she was not smart enough—did not have the aptitude—to do chemistry. She began to critique that belief and the power structure that had imposed that definition on her with the support of some of the students through our oral histories. Gene and Laurie seemed to have similar experiences as they rethought their own science experiences (Gene's experiences, of course, being rather different from Laurie's or Tracy's because he started our class liking science "at its core"). Through critiquing science from the standpoint of their own lived experiences, these students point out that in having an awareness of the positionality that we bring to relationships, we also have a better understanding of how the power arrangements influence such relationships in science. It is through rereading our lives (and our lived experiences) and using the knowledge of power arrangements that such changes can occur and allow us to begin to reposition ourselves in science and education.

REFLECTIONS

I learned through conversations with my students over the summer that some of them had developed and acted upon a critical awareness of the science in their lives. The connections that Laurie, Tracy, and Gene made between concepts in science, critiques of science, and their lived experiences were connections that I did not expect; connections that I did not know how to consider. I knew that Gene was a high school science teacher, but I had not considered that sharing with the students my struggles to teach science through a liberatory agenda and meeting the requirements and responsibilities of the college would parallel (in some ways) Gene's own struggles at the high school level. I also knew that Tracy wanted to study social work, but had not thought about why she actively resisted psychology as a science. Listening and learning from my students, as they developed a critical awareness of the science in their lives and of the theoretical tools needed to make sense of it, I recognized my own need to foster that kind of conversation as part of my pedagogical practice in science class. If I wanted to help students make connections between their lived experiences, science, critiques of science, and oppression and privilege, I needed to create opportunities for a class conversation that allowed the students to talk about their struggles. I needed to value the kinds of conversations that allowed for the full range of our lived experiences in our class, and I had to do so in ways that did not set up a fixed oppositional discourse: science or nonscience voices, male or female voices.

By pushing me to consider their interpretations of our class, these students emphasized the situational nature of knowledge, the situational nature of relationships. Our places in class as students, teacher, male, female, minority, or working class, and the ways in which these places are embedded into the power structures active in our class, created different contexts from which to make meaning in class. Tracy, at the end of the semester, firmly believed that much of what we did in our class was "not science" and that her intended major, psychology (in the context of social work), was "not science." These things were fun, and valued her ideas and experiences, and therefore were not science. It became obvious to me that Tracy had learned to critique the institution of science and how it defined her, but possessed no overt desire or energy to try to revision it.

These summer conversational meetings were important in helping me to revision a more interactive pedagogy for the future. Central to this was the shift in my role from teacher to colearner (Hollingsworth, 1994b). During the summer, the power relation changed, as I no longer held the students' "chemistry fate" in my hands. Furthermore, my stance as learner and as one who needed the conversation of others to learn reaffirmed our equal footing. The opportunity to talk with students allowed me to rethink my teaching and my reflections from their perspectives. I believe that our conversations provided a place for us to continue the conversations we had begun in class about science, education, society, ideology, and our lives, as a way for all of us to continue to learn how we shape science, how science shapes us, and how we can change the way we shape science. Through these conversations, we all learned more about ourselves and science education.

The summer conversations helped me to see the agency in positionality. In the spring, as with the oral histories, positionality helped me to understand how our lived experiences shaped our understanding of science and our attitudes about science. But because my teacher research is firmly grounded in my political commitment to push for social justice in science and education, my understanding of positionality and how it influences my teaching and my students' learning in science is important but not enough. This understanding needs to be put into action to revision a living science education.

I thus see these summer conversations as a transition period in my own orientation towards a feminist liberatory education in science. Through my students' interventions, I learned that their ability to deconstruct the hierarchical relationship between science and nonscience, or insider and outsider, and to struggle against the boundaries imposed by the pervasive political agenda of science and education were grounded in our commitment to give voice to their marginalized and silenced experiences in science.

When I was teaching in the spring, I did not understand the importance of allowing the students to share their stories of their lives as they connected with the oral histories or the subject matter knowledge conversations. I realized that their stories were a powerful witness to the political and ideological dimensions of science and how science shapes our lives in positive and negative ways. Yet I constantly wrestled with the fact that some of their stories seemed very distant from the critiques that I wanted to share and even more distant from the subject matter knowledge that we were required to learn in the course. What I recognize through my experience with the summer conversations is that by creating spaces in our chemistry class for students to share their lived experiences in multiple contexts (Lisa Karms, Dr. Phillips), we were also learning together how our multiple positionings in the world had shaped our experiences in science and hence our ideas about and relationships in it. We were learning to rearticulate the meanings imposed on our experiences. As a feminist science educator, I thus recognized how the interventions by my students widened my vision of how positionality can contribute to feminist science education. It is not just a theoretical construct I can use to understand what we do, but a dynamic set of relationships that we can explore to interrogate our understandings in science.

5

Centering Lived Experience

In the two previous chapters, I have raised questions about how students and teachers co-construct science and the self in that science. Feminists argue that this construction process is influenced by many things, including traditional images of science projected by textbooks, the media, and even the scientific community. When the perpetrators of these images neglect to acknowledge the multiple ways in which students and teachers as individuals intersect or do not intersect with these dominant images, often students, and even sometimes science teachers, turn away from this science that has silenced their experiences, values, and beliefs. The idea that students and teachers play an active role in the process of constructing science and the self in that science points to the political dimensions of positionality and feminist science education. In the second chapter, I suggested that positionality is political because it refers to the relational space people occupy within a set of sociopolitical relationships and that the ways in which relational spaces are understood and even constructed reflect and reproduce the power dynamics active within society. It also refers to the implications that making explicit the situated nature of knowledge and understanding have for schooling or any other institutionalized practice. In this chapter, I explore the political dimensions of positionality in science class through the act of centering lived experience in science class or, in other words, making lived experience as much of an issue in science class as the science itself. I also explore the implications that centering lived experiences has for how science and scientific knowledge are defined in science education, and the dilemmas this raises for teachers who practice this. To do so, I relate two brief stories from my science teaching. Each story describes my attempts to create a learning environment that would allow the students to build a critical understanding of Western science as well as of the identities, beliefs, and values traditionally attached to the roles we are taught to play in science class as scientists, teachers, and students. The first story, ''To Talk About Juan's Mother or Not,'' reflects the dilemmas imposed by centering experience in science class. The second story, "Midwives, Science and Intuitive Scientific Knowledge," illustrates how the act of centering experience in science class helps students to challenge content construction and whose ideas count as science.

TO TALK ABOUT JUAN'S MOTHER OR NOT

Doing Atomic Theory with the Cyclotron

Toward the middle of the semester, I had my chemistry class immersed in a unit on atomic theory. As part of our study of atomic theory, we had taken a field trip to one of the most powerful cyclotrons in the world (which happened to be located at one of the nearby universities). My reasons for arranging this field trip were fourfold. First, I wanted to locate our study physically. We were in the midst of a unit where we were taking a historical approach to understanding the development of the atom. I wanted the students to be exposed to the equipment and laboratory processes used to construct information about atoms. Such equipment is too expensive for most universities, let alone our community college. Consequently, the exposure that chemistry students typically have to atomic theory lies solely in what different books or articles can share two-dimensionally. Second, I wanted to locate atomic theory research socially and culturally. I wanted the students to know that these researchers had real and situational motivations for constructing their research design and interpretation schemes the way they did. I wanted my students to have the chance to ask them questions about that, too. My third reason was that I wanted to impose on us a situation that would force us to articulate our connections and alienations from science. In the cyclotron, a great deal of fancy equipment and language are used to research highly abstract ideas (how long does it take a single, isolated krypton atom to lose all of its electrons?) as well as directly applicable ideas (can an intense stream of neutrons be used effectively in localized treatment of soft tissue cancers?). These sorts of intellectual-emotional confrontations might create contexts in which to engage in conversations that would expose for critique the connections and divergences between students' experiences and assumptions about the accessibility of knowledge and practice of Western science. My final reason was that I, myself, had completed graduate studies in quantum mechanics, and I found this kind of theory and practice on the atomic level fascinating. I wanted to work proactively to dissolve some of the barriers, such as language and access to knowledge, that make this work inaccessible to community college students. I wanted to help my students to negotiate their way through the discourse of science—a discourse not intended for most of my students because of their social locations (Lewis & Simon, 1986)—with confidence and with a critical perspective.

During our visit to the cyclotron, many interesting conversations came to the fore. For example, the tour guide—a cyclotron physicist—described a current study designed to measure the length of time it would take to strip a krypton atom of all its electrons at a given energy level. He boasted that this 2-week study cost two million dollars. An older student, Paula, asked the physicist why this particular research was being conducted. His response was "because it is fun . . . it really has no application." Later, when the class was alone, Paula raised this issue again by questioning the class about the multiple ways in which the two million krypton dollars could be spent. Another example involved our class discussion about how the cyclotron equipment, when taken by itself, can be intimidating. This conversation was initiated by my requesting their responses to the physical structures of the cyclotron—large, complicated-looking equipment with tons of wires, computers, and indecipherable pieces of metal and plastic.

Although these two conversations yielded fascinating insights and emotional debates for my students and myself about the nature of chemistry in a cyclotron, the uses and abuses of basic research, and the vast amounts of money spent for 2 weeks of work, the conversation I would like to focus on briefly was one surrounding the only practical application to emerge from the cyclotron research at this university (that we were allowed to learn about): the medical cyclotron. We learned in our visit that the researchers at this university had applied their ability to create single-neutron-wide beams to treat soft tissue cancer, and we learned how the process worked on the atomic level. This procedure had been hailed in specific forms of brain cancer treatment for its ability to locally, yet radically, treat tumors. What was even more exciting about this approach was that because it had been developed at the local university, this kind of cancer treatment was being pioneered almost exclusively at one of the area hospital cancer facilities, with remarkable success.

Because this was the only apparent positive connection between the specific research at this cyclotron and everyday life, and because I believed that any attempts to politicize connections and divergences between students' experiences and beliefs must contain elements of possibility, in a conversation following our tour, I elicited students' stories and experiences in connection to this topic. It was during this time that Juan, a recent immigrant to the United States, raised the politically and socially drenched question of why his mother—when she was dying of the same kind of cancer described by the cyclotron researcher— did not receive this treatment, even though she lived relatively close to the medical cyclotron. He told the class that his mother's cancer was emotionally and physically painful, and that she was consistently told by her health care provider that there was nothing that could be done.

The reaction to Juan's story about his mother was mixed: Several students vocally expressed sympathy for his mother's illness ("Juan, I am so sorry!"). Other students expressed a disbelief that this could happen in the United States ("No way! Juan, did that really happen?"). In the conversation that ensued, many students began to tell their own stories about their experiences of inadequacy from the medical profession. Others asked questions about the legality of access to health care and experimental medical research. These questions, raised by the students, helped to create a space for us to talk about (1) what we knew about how the medical cyclotron worked (which is integrally related to an understanding of atomic theory), and (2) how this knowledge was sought through culturally motivated channels. We learned that the medical cyclotron is used in soft tissue cancers and, specifically, in prostate and brain cancers. Soft tissue cancers, however, include breast cancer. Student questions and concerns about medical research and Juan's mother guided us to the question, Why is the medical cyclotron used in prostate and brain cancers and not in breast cancer? Our talk about the medical cyclotron allowed me to guide the students to integrate an understanding of how the medical cyclotron works with larger issues of knowledge construction, power relations, and lived experience.

Dilemmas of Centering Lived Experience

Juan's story, in many ways, was just the kind of thing that I, as a feminist teacher-researcher, wanted a student to say: It was provocative. It challenged institutional structures in science and medicine and their effects on our lives. It gave a context to the struggle to help students realize that science is a social and cultural process with social and cultural ramifications. Yet Juan's story unleashed a conversation about power, control, knowledge, and position that I felt ill prepared to handle. I did not know "the facts" surrounding his mother's struggle with cancer. Was she really denied effective health care? I also struggled to see connections between atomic theory, Juan's mother, and the possibility for liberatory education: How did talking about Juan's mother make the study of atomic theory any more "liberating"?

Ignoring Juan's story meant ignoring his lived experiences and losing a possibility to politicize the connections and divergences between his experiences and assumptions about the accessibility of knowledge and practice of Western science. Yet pursuing Juan's story, as we did, meant engaging in a discourse on the politics of poverty, sexism, and racism in the health care system, which clearly seems outside the boundaries of a typical chemistry class. Therefore, constructively addressing these kinds of experiences that the students brought embraces an overtly political pedagogy. Why is it that Juan's mother did not receive aggressive treatment for her cancer? What is it about the politics of poverty, race, and gender that contribute to inconsistencies in the health care systems? Although Juan's experience was useful in helping the rest of the students not just understand the science but also critique why learning that science made them feel disconnected and alienated, the challenges inherent in a science education built on the political dimensions of a critical scientific literacy are many: Is it possible not to hierarchically locate students' experiences? How can a critical scientific literacy stay focused on science? Or, ought it stay focused on science?

The story of Juan's mother and the medical cyclotron illustrates how knowledge about science developed in our class grew out of the students' interests and backgrounds, which are highly individual and culture specific. Central to constructing new knowledge in class about cyclotrons, atomic theory, and medical treatment was an opportunity for students to articulate their own understandings of how these ideas or technologies intersected with their lives. The ways in which our lives connected to or diverged from these ideas and technologies became integral to learning about them. This is an important point when considering how a feminist lens can help to politicize science teaching in a way that allows for student movement and growth because it integrates epistemological and ideological questions with human interaction and institutional power arrangements. It is one thing to help students conceptually understand science from the standpoints of their own lives. It is quite another to help them use that personal knowledge to understand, then critique, a powerfully long-standing and excluding discipline. This starting point is important in creating a critical scientific literacy for all students because it starts from the experiences of the students, and uses their knowledge to build a critical understanding of science as well as of their own experiences.

MIDWIVES, SCIENCE, AND INTUITIVE SCIENTIFIC KNOWLEDGE

Ann's Oral History Report on the Life of Martha Ballard

Late in the spring semester, as part of a history project component of our chemistry class,[1] Ann, a young, quiet, white woman and an occupational therapy major, shared her report on the life of Martha Ballard,[2] a midwife who lived and worked during the late 1700s and the early 1800s. Ann's main points were that Martha developed her understanding of science and of her practice through personal experience and observation, and that prevailing social norms made midwifery political in nature during the late 1700s and early 1800s.

After Ann nervously shared her ideas with the class, the students debated questions about the nature of science: How could the work of Martha Ballard be characterized? What does it mean to know and do science? Did Martha do science? Or, as John asked, "What does [Martha Ballard's] occupation have to do with science?" Martha Ballard's life provided the students with a context from which to talk about the nature of science as we entertained these largely philosophical questions. Martha had no formal training in the sciences, but learned a great deal through observation and personal research with the medicinal herbs she cultivated at home. When challenged with the authenticity of Martha's scientific practice, Ann defensively informed the class, "[Martha] didn't have any formal training; she never went to school. What she knew about science or about medicine, she learned by herself. She learned a lot just by being one of the only midwives in the area. I think the book said that she took care of hundreds of people. She also learned a lot just by observation and doing."

As we searched for answers about what it means to know and do science through Martha Ballard's lived experiences, our discussion shifted from Martha's lifework in science to ways in which we knew science:

> ANN: Men monopolize business, medical doctors, and other stuff. Women are treated as property and as baby makers. She [Martha] would receive letters from women who were pregnant, then she would go help them through labor and spend all her time there till the baby was born. Women were noticed as nobodies, even as a midwife. In my opinion, women would know more about giving birth even by experience and not by schooling. Men were the main people in science and women were not sought to be scientists and doctors. Midwives were

the highest women could be. Martha did not agree with that, and I do not agree with that either.

JOHN: What does her occupation have to do with science?

ANN: She delivered babies. She saw herself as a scientist because she brought the babies into the world.

ANDREA: Did she have any training?

ANN: (Defensively) She didn't have any formal training; she never went to school. What she knew about science or about medicine, she learned by herself. She learned a lot just by being one of the only midwives in the area. I think the book said that she took care of hundreds of people. She also learned a lot just by observation and doing.

ANDREA: But what happens if something went wrong? Would she have to call a doctor? It seems to me that without school she couldn't handle an emergency.

DESHAWN: (With apparent frustration) I think they have learned a lot through experience. Experience was their education. Just because she didn't go to school just like the men could go to school, doesn't mean that she didn't understand what she was doing.

VAL: (Interrupting DeShawn) Men don't know the experience of having a baby.

DESHAWN: (Continuing where she left off) We've poopooed a lot of old wives' tales. Going through experiences and making our own assumptions and observations is important. It sounds like Martha learned a lot about medicine that way. She grew her herbs and made up her own medicine. There are probably a lot of old wives' tales that really work, but people just don't listen because they are not doctors.

VAL: I have four children and every time I have gone to the hospital to give birth, the doctors have always treated me as if I were an object. They seemed to care more about their doctoring and their fancy equipment and with the fact that they have to deliver a baby than the idea that I am there struggling to give birth. I probably know more than they do about some of the things related to having a baby, just because I have experienced it four times.

ALLERIA: (To teacher) Yeah, but is it better to be treated as an object and to not have problems or to be treated like a human and have something go wrong?

ANDREA: I'd rather go to a hospital. I wouldn't want anything to go wrong if I were going to have a baby.

LYNN: You are assuming that by having a baby with a midwife, something will go wrong. Most births, either inside or outside the hospital, happen without any of the major problems. Besides, a midwife probably is capable of handling a lot of problems. Like Martha Ballard, is that her name?—she was able to deal with a lot, because she spent time doing that kind of thing.

ALLERIA: Yeah, that's true, I am just saying—

RON: (Interrupting) Would you be more apt to sue a male doctor or a midwife?

DESHAWN: (To Ron) Not all doctors are male.

RON: (To DeShawn) You are making this into a man-woman thing.

DESHAWN: (To Ron) I am not, I just want to point out that you were assuming that the midwife was a woman and the doctor a man. (April 18, 1994)[3]

As this segment of our classroom conversation indicates, our talk about the nature of science developed into a discussion on how many members of the class already intuitively knew a great deal of science through everyday activities that some of us needed or were required to perform—childbirth and health. Although John and Ron attempted to defend traditional science, the women's comments pushed against the limitations of the abstract nature of chemical concepts and its relationship to the practices of those scientists who have chosen to name the world in ways discontinuous with their own lived experiences. For example, Val and Ann pushed their peers to reconsider childbirth, personal knowledge, and science. Val was a Latina mother of four, full-time caregiver in her family, part-time worker, and part-time student. Val cherished her duties as a mother and caregiver. She felt that it was her duty as a Christian woman and mother to take responsibility for the care of her children.[4] As she wrote in her journal toward the beginning of the semester, "I do not really like science, and I have never had the chance to study it. I need to take care of my children. That gets in the way of school, but they are worth it and that is what I like to do." These multiple and contradictory roles gave Val a unique position from which to explore what she knew about herself and about her world and how that knowledge was valued in particular situations.

Ann also brought an interesting set of lived experiences to the conversation that helped her shape our talk in interesting ways. For several years, she had been working as a receptionist's aid in a doctor's office. She suffered from chronic asthma and as a result, spent a great deal of time at the hospital in out-patient treatment. These experiences certainly gave her a great deal of contact with the medical community and some insight into what it means to exist with that community as a semi-insider (receptionist) and as an outsider (patient and receptionist).

Later in the conversation, in addition to focusing on the nature of science, several students, both male and female, developed the theme of the political nature of medicine originally presented by Ann: Martha was not valued by the medical doctors in her community because she was a midwife and a woman, even though her practice was as extensive as theirs and perhaps more physically and emotionally demanding. These challenges to the traditional practice of science continued to be refuted by Ron. The class explored this theme by discussing it in relation to current issues in health care. The following transcript excerpt illustrates this point well:

> MARK J.: I think part of the way that doctors treat you is related to hospitals being businesses. They are out there just like everyone else trying to make money.
>
> MARK L.: (Nodding in agreement) It's hard to tell with a hospital because who are hospitals for now, anyway? They are just businesses now. Nobody really cares about the patients, they just have to get the money and make a profit.
>
> RICK: (Sounding frustrated) But some of those doctors have been to school for at least 11 years. That's got to mean something.
>
> LYNN: Have you ever noticed that women doctors pay more attention to you?
>
> MARK L.: (Responding to Rick) Well, I—medical science is too commercialized to be objective.
>
> LYNN: Oh I know, how they treat you is all based on insurance.
>
> ANN: That's true; because I have asthma, and sometimes I need to go to the hospital for treatment and I spend more time doing stuff for insurance before they even will see me, than I do with the doctor.
>
> LYNN: Medicine is all about money. That's kind of depressing because I want to go into medical research, and I just wonder what it will be like.

As the transcript indicates, the students began to articulate the notion that doctoring has become an economically and politically motivated profession. "Medicine is all about money"; it is just a "business" with an emphasis on "making money" rather than on treating people. In so doing, the students expressed standpoints critical of science as an institution. They began to critique the socially acceptable belief that midwifery is only a "*nonscience* science," whereas doctoring is a "*science science.*" What are particularly interesting are the kinds of experiences and ideas that pushed particular students to take such a critical stand. Several of the women (Lynn, Val, and Ann) were immediately critical when the class discussed how people are treated in doctors' offices. Some of the men (Mark L. and Mark J.) began to articulate a critical standpoint when business issues were raised.

The conversation about Martha Ballard, science, politics, and personal experience left a vivid imprint on me as a feminist teacher-researcher interested in positionality. After hearing Ann's presentation, I expected the students' discussion to focus on the question, Who was considered a scientist and who was not? I was curious to learn more about how the students would grapple with this question, especially after having been presented with pieces of the dynamic life of Martha Ballard. But hearing the students struggle with knowing science in ways that were at once similar to, and yet different from, traditional ways of knowing science as a result of lived experiences pointed toward new connections between the experiences of my students and science. Indeed, I was surprised by the intensity with which the students wanted to define their own knowledge, and with how problematic that process was for them. Val struggled with finding a place to define her own science when she shared her experiences of feeling like an "object" while giving birth. This struggle with defining knowledge was also evident in DeShawn's ideas about how midwives learn science through experience.

The opposing tension—a fear or unwillingness to define their own knowledge—was articulated by Andrea when she asked sincerely and with concern, "But what happens if something went wrong? Would she have to call a doctor? It seems to me that without school she couldn't handle an emergency," and when she declared that if faced with childbirth, "I'd rather go to the hospital. I wouldn't want anything to go wrong if I were going to have a baby." This tension was also evident in Alleria's comment, "Yeah, but is it better to be treated as an object and to not have problems or to be treated like a human and have something go wrong?"

These issues raised by the students significantly impacted the definition of science made public by the students. Up until this conversation, during our semester together, the students never so explicitly nor so passionately defined for me their (dis)connections with science. The "liberatory focus" thus had been on the more superficial attempts to find connections between the students' experiences and science or by trying to build a "new" science built on the experiences of the women and minorities. This conversation, however, began to politicize how our social locations shaped the relationships that the students and I created with each other and with science, and how this ultimately influenced how we defined ourselves and our knowledge. This conversation created an uncomfortable tension between personal experiences in science and the science of the educational institution. At that particular moment, as both teacher and scientist, I felt that our conversation had certainly changed the dynamics of what we were doing in class, especially since most students were in the class to prepare for future careers in health (respiratory and occupational therapists, home health care specialists, registered nurses, and licensed practical nurses).

Dilemmas of Challenging Science Through Experience

This conversation raises several questions about positionality and its connection to liberatory education in science: What did it mean to understand or challenge traditional science or to create a new science when who we were as students of science, as (non) participants in science, did not interact with the world view of science? What was the nature of the relationship that existed between the students, chemistry, and myself and how did this bound (if at all) our vision of chemistry, of science, and of our relationships with and in science? Could we politicize these relationships so that they could become a source of understanding, critique, and revisioning rather than of potential oppression?

My retrospective reading of the Martha Ballard conversation suggests that the students and I shared ideas and experiences that explained and confronted how societal, economic, and political agendas influence science and our relationships with science and with each other in science. I recognize that these ideas were not explored in depth with the students or even in connection to the chemistry we were to learn that day after the oral history conversation. However, many of the students explored how science could be learned through experience and observation rather than as traditional abstracted school knowledge. Ron's very vocal support for traditional science notwithstanding, many of the members of the class expressed that they felt controlled by science because of their physical circumstances as women and as nonscientists, even when they felt that their experiences warranted their participation in science. This idea was clearly evident in Val's comment about the birthing process and modern medicine.

The Martha Ballard conversation helped me as a teacher to see how the possibilities for feminist liberatory education are connected to the kinds of relationships that are constructed and valued in science class as well as to the ways in which these relationships are talked about and examined in the public space of the science class. It helped me to see that a revisioned science begins with the repositioning of the traditional power-knowledge relationships that influence how students learn to label valued knowledge. The conversation reflects this idea: By our valuing childbirth experiences and bringing them into the class conversation, the authority of Western science was partially demystified and decentered. Centering Val's, Ann's, and Martha Ballard's experiences changed the way science was viewed and experienced in our class. In a very small way, the students challenged relationships marked by power hierarchies such as the nonscientist-scientist, by publicly examining their own positions in science class. This conversation gave me hope that it was possible to interrogate the master narratives in science, which legitimate the dominant standard and simultaneously delegitimize any other perspective as "nonstandard" and "nonwhole."

The Martha Ballard conversation gave my class a language and a space in which to resist and refuse the alienating practices of science that they had experienced through the promotion of science as nonsubjective—removed from personal, social, political, and historical experiences in their lives or the lives of others. The students and I experienced what it meant to live our knowledge in science class, as did Martha Ballard and Val, rather then to appropriate it abstractly. Martha Ballard, along with several students, helped us all to think critically about our lives as science teachers and learners, men and women, caregivers and patients, by insisting that we claim our life experiences as valuable knowledge.

TRANSFORMING EDUCATION THROUGH POLITICAL PEDAGOGICAL PRACTICE

Education represents both a struggle for meaning and a struggle over power relations. Thus education becomes a central terrain where power and politics operate out of the lived culture of the individuals and groups situated in asymmetrical social and political positions. This way of understanding the academy entails a critique of education as the mere accumulation of disciplinary knowledges that can be exchanged on the world market for upward mobility. (Mohanty, 1994, p. 147)

Science class is a complex social site marked by multiple interacting layers of power arrangements and social and institutional forces that shape and define the boundaries of what is possible. Chandra Talpade

Mohanty (1994) argues for a political and transforming vision of education. From the perspective of a feminist science teacher-researcher, science education is about more than passing on the disciplinary knowledge of science. This political and critical view of education suggests that education is about issues of power and relationships. As Weiler (1988) suggests, "Teaching extends beyond subject matter knowledge; the centrality of teaching lies in a recognition of the values of students' own voices, subjective experiences of power and oppression, and the worth of their class and ethnic cultures" (p. 148). Thus, one goal of science education must be to raise questions and issues with students that unsettle the accepted social realities in the science classroom and in science.

Feminist science teaching takes place within the wider cultural and institutional structures of school and science that bound our visions of teaching, learning, science, and selves. Juxtaposing the Martha Ballard class conversation with Juan's story points to a need to politicize these structures as part of my pedagogical practice in science class. If students are to make connections between their lived experiences, science, critiques of science, and oppression and privilege, opportunities for the students to talk about their struggles need to be created in ways that do not set up a fixed oppositional discourses.

Thus, one central issue that emerges in the Martha Ballard and Juan stories is the notion of using the lived experiences of classroom participants as locations for politicizing the connections and divergences between different ways of knowing and doing. More specifically, these stories suggest that inclusive and liberatory science educations are made possible through valuing the students' home cultures and personal experiences, and by making explicit and accessible to all students the cultural capital of traditional science knowledge and school-based knowledge. To make a science inclusive of "all," the science experiences of those not traditionally endorsed by status quo practices must be validated, and connections and divergences between such experiences and "real science" must be made explicit. Making explicit these connections and divergences creates contexts from which students and teachers can reread the science in their lives and their lives in science.

This process is complex because talking, doing, and reading science in our lives are shaped by interrelated gender, race, and class texts. However, the process of politicizing connections and divergences provides spaces in which to critique and revision. This critique and revision can take many shapes. Teachers and students can work together to explicitly rename seemingly predefined school knowledge from their perspectives so that their perspectives and voices became their knowledge. For example, science class talk about the birthing process became more than learning how to fit lived experience inside of science to explain science. Instead, talking about this became the students' science, whether or not it was in accord with traditional science. In the cyclotron story, our study of atomic theory was shaped by the existing needs to understand and to critique medical cyclotron research.

Students and teachers can also rename their relationship to the traditional content and process of science. In the Martha Ballard conversation the students' and my actions contributed to making our relationships with the institutions of science and education problematic. Ann, DeShawn, and Val created possibilities for our class community to explore the relationships we have with and in science when these women articulated their views about the life of Martha Ballard. Juan's story provided the students and me with a space to rename our relationships to the traditional content and process of science. The conversation about access to the medical profession opened up an opportunity for us to discuss what we knew about atomic theory and why the research has been guided in specific directions and made accessible only to specific people.

Attempting to articulate and highlight the complexity of the students' lives, which has traditionally been silenced by science and science education, and then publicly reconstructing a relationship with science and with each other in science class that embodies and reflects such complexity constitutes an effort to reinvent relationships with science. It constitutes an effort to reshape the power arrangements in science class by decentering the omnipotence of traditional Western science.

The issues that I have raised about science and education are central to my efforts to understand the possibilities for liberatory education. I believe that these efforts will help to construct ways to uncover the grand narratives that structure thinking and learning in schools. Yet I am left with many unanswered questions. In my science teaching-researching, I often worry that, because I teach my students to value their lived experiences as their science and to challenge traditional science from the standpoints of their lives, I am actively helping to keep a wall between science and people who are silenced in science. I wonder if the act of building new and more liberatory relationships in science is helping to perpetuate the "being in" and the "being out" of science, despite my efforts to blur these dichotomies.

These questions and concerns are not new, especially in the context of critical, feminist, and poststructural theories; they are a reminder of the unintended consequences of liberatory teaching and learning.

Reflecting on possible consequences has helped me to look beyond wondering how to teach students how to act and talk on the margin and at the center and to consider instead how science teaching and learning might be revisioned in ways that implode the center/margin barriers. If instead of stepping over barriers or crossing borders students could move freely from margin to center and back again, margins might not continue to be otherized. How might that be accomplished? Well, it might mean different approaches for different groups of students. For example, the adult students I worked with, because they are adults, might be able to confront issues of power more easily than might younger students. Even if children do begin to use science to act on their world and even if they do use their cultural and lived experiences to challenge institutionalized science, they are yet children, and the power that adults in their lives hold over them may not be lightly mitigated. On the other hand, issues of position might more easily be addressed with younger students, who have not yet accumulated as much baggage associated with "appropriate" roles for women and men as adults likely have. If the goal of liberatory education is to help students bring their lives to their education and in turn use their education to act on their lives, our responsibility as teachers, I believe, demands that we help our students to identify and dissolve those institutional barriers that slow their journey.

6

Revisioning Science Through Lived Experience

> When our lived experience of theorizing is fundamentally linked to the process of self-recovery, of collective liberation, no gap exists between theory and practice. Indeed, what such experience makes more evident is the bond between the two—that ultimately reciprocal process wherein one enables the other.
>
> —bell hooks, *Teaching to Transgress*

Feminists have challenged the universal subject and disciplinary truths in science (Fox Keller, 1985; Harding, 1991) and in science education (Stanley & Brickhouse, 1995; WISE, 1995). This rejection of a foundational epistemology in science and science education calls for a transformed subject that challenges singular ways of knowing or being in science. This has wide-ranging implications for science education. It challenges the canon that science teachers have been charged to teach. It challenges the ways in which students are expected to claim (or not to claim) that canon for their own. It challenges the kinds of research that we do on how teachers teach and how students learn the subject of science. My own study through the lens of positionality of what it could mean to teach a feminist liberatory science education exposes this argument. As I have suggested, students' experiences, like the canon of science, cannot be taken for granted, and they cannot be left to lie untouched behind the tails of a universalistic subject of science. Juan and his mother, Val and her children, Tracy, Gene, and Laurie, and our conversations, all give witness to the ways in which critical examination of lived experiences leads to the breakdown of the universal subject and the knowledge-power nexus in science and science education.

LEARNING SCIENCE THROUGH WHOSE EXPERIENCES?

The idea of "critical examination of lived experience" is central to this argument. Progressive educators historically have attempted to help students understand and connect to science by explaining scientific phenomenon through "real world" experiences. Reform initiatives in science education rely on the use of personal experience because it has been shown to help students to grasp science better, to have more positive attitudes about science, and to understand how science applies to their own lives (AAAS, 1989, 1993; National Research Council [NRC], 1996). This is significant. However, the feminist critique of the universal subject and my own understanding of what happens when positionality is made to be an issue in science class has led to a particular analysis of this action. When science educators use personal experience to help students understand science, or to explain science, or to make science more real, there is a hierarchical ranking placed on the value of students' particular experiences. Specifically, those out-of-school experiences that are deemed acceptable in science class (i.e., the ones that fit neatly with the kinds of concepts taught) are more highly valued than those deemed unacceptable. As feminist researchers (Roychoudhury, Tippins, & Nichols, 1995; WISE, 1995) remind us, this has historically favored the boys because of their experiences with machines, construction, and the world of work and men's bodies. Critical theorists (Apple, 1979, 1992, 1994; Giroux, 1985; Willis, 1977) remind us that schooling, moreover, favors children in families with financial and educational resources. In physics classrooms, teachers (and children) talk about bicycle pumps, toasters, and electrical wiring systems in studying thermodynamics and electromagnetism. Questions that have been raised by feminist include, What happens when children do not have experiences with these kinds of things? How will they connect to the scientific knowledge base? Consequently, there has been a movement geared towards creating a gender- and culture-sensitive or inclusive science education (Atwater, 1996; Roychoudhury, Tippins, & Nichols, 1995). These movements have been crucial in helping to create equitable opportunities for all students to develop scientific literacy.

TWISTING EXPERIENCES INTO SCIENCE

Another question surrounding the use of experience in science class has grown out of feminist studies in science education: How are students' lived experiences used, manipulated, forced, pulled, and tugged to *fit within the confines of science?* In the enthusiasm to help students develop understandings of scientific principles, concepts, and processes, there exists a forgetfulness of the idea that students, like all human beings, come to understand the world through multiple and intersecting lenses. Even when students compartmentalize understandings, there are many persistent linkages between compartments. As a result, students' readings of their experiences often do not fit neatly or fully those prescribed experiences located within the borders of science. Valuing lived experience and their complexities and idiosyncrasies challenges "neat science." They implode the boundaries that separate science from nonscience. This raises several significant questions that I will explore in this chapter: What happens to science and official scientific knowledge if students' lived experiences are valued in their complexities? How does this influence the self-in-science?

The students whom I write about in this book are community college students. Many are single mothers who hold working-class jobs. Many of them have deep concerns about their children. Not only have they experienced childbirth, they are also the primary caregivers. As such, they are responsible on a daily basis for cooking and cleaning and for playing with, disciplining, and instilling values in their children. This point is significant, because much of what these students do outside of science class does not involve the kinds of things that have traditionally been valued in science class. For example, the role of caregiver—teaching children to read, cook, clean, and care for themselves, changing diapers, cleaning wounds—involves many activities that are never mentioned in science texts in ways that would embody these acts as the heart of science (Osborne, 1995). Many excellent teachers have brought some of these activities into science class to explain certain phenomena such as bacterial infections or chemical reactions. However, it is the act of bringing science to an arena where the complex role of caregiver is central, instead of bringing the work of caregiver to the arena where science is central (and hence the dominant and identifying source) that makes the use of lived experience both political and radical. And it is the critical examination of these lived experiences that pushes away from universalizing the role of caregiver, or as postcritical critique reminds us, exchanging the truth regime of science for a truth regime of another sort. This raises serious implications for creating science from the students' lived experiences, because such experiences are not neatly categorized into science. If only the dimensions of the experiences that neatly fit into science are valued, whereas the other dimensions are ignored, science remains the central force through which students are

expected to define themselves. Opportunities for understanding, analyzing, and re-creating science from multiple perspectives is minimized.
I am not arguing that science as it is now should not be understood as it
is now. It must be by all students, for that is one key to gaining access to
the cultural capital that is required to be a force within that community.
As Delpit (1988) argues, educators cannot deny how knowledge of the
canon, no matter how oppressive, serves as a gate to the culture of
power, and thus the possibility for changing that culture of power.
What I am arguing, therefore, is that helping students to understand
science as it is now, without an analytical element that draws its
strength from multiple standpoints, diminishes the importance of all
that stands outside of the imposed boundaries of Western science. It
diminishes the focus on science as a subjective activity, one that is filled
with intention and value. Let us return to my chemistry class to make
sense of these issues.

REVISIONING SCIENCE THROUGH EXPERIENCE: GAS LAWS

In mid-April of 1994, about halfway through chemistry class, the students and I had just finished discussing the relationships between the
four variables, temperature, pressure, volume, and amount, in ideal
gases (the "gas laws"). This conversation was based on an earlier group
assignment where the students explored ways in which they knew
things about gases through their lives at home and at work. I gave this
assignment because I wanted to introduce the students at a later point
to the canonically accepted gas laws, and I wanted them to have an
articulated knowledge base about it that was connected to their experiences. I felt this was particularly important because in my department,
the gas laws have historically been an area of chemistry where students
have performed poorly. The variety of ways that students were able to
draw connections between the four variables were diverse: Gloria and
Beth talked about how they understood the relationship between pressure, volume, and amount of gases because of Beth's 7-year-old son's
whoopee cushion. Juan and Sol talked about how they understood the
relationships between pressure, volume, and temperature through
working on automobile tires at home and at work. Linda, Reana, Mag-
gie, Holia, Rico, and Bill related temperature and pressure to their experiences with cooking.

Linda, an older woman returning to school because she "wanted
something different out of life," brought in material required for cooking spaghetti to explain some things about gases. It is important to note

at this point that Linda is a "good" student: She read the textbook that the department chair had selected for our course and solved the problems in the chapter despite the fact that we did not follow the textbook very closely and that this was not an activity required in my course. Linda described to the class how, in one of her first attempts to cook spaghetti, she filled a pot with water, let the water boil, placed the spaghetti in the water, put the top on the pot, and walked away with the intention of returning to the stove in 10 minutes to drain the spaghetti. But, she said, her cooking plans did not go as smoothly as she'd thought they would. As she sat at her table reading a magazine, she heard a crash from the stove. The top of the pot had been pushed off. She noticed that there were "tons of bubbles overflowing the pot" (which she interpreted as bubbles of gas created by the water boiling). She said that she then realized that boiling water required more room; it "sort of needed a way to let some of the gas to escape." She understood the boiling water as having pushed the top off the pot because the top was limiting the room that the boiling water needed. Now, she said, she cooks spaghetti with the top "half on and half off" so that the boiling water has a place to go. She then made a connection between heating the water (temperature), the top moving off (pressure) and the amount of space needed (volume), and how they affected one another in different ways depending on "what was happening at the time."

In the course of the conversation, Linda expressed to her group her surprise with her own understanding of gases. She had learned from her experience that heat, size, and pressure are related. She had learned that she could make informed and intellectual decisions based on her own theories. Later, when I read her journal, I found that she had developed these ideas "long ago" and had used this knowledge several times since, but had never thought of her ideas as "science" and, in particular, had never thought of them as "abstract." She just thought of them as "common sense about cooking." This is important because *abstract* was something that Linda said was clearly the message she had received from the author of the textbook when reading his presentation of gas laws.

It is interesting to note that what happened in class was a result of the tension caused by her experience of not neatly fitting into the science in the text. When Linda described her understanding of pressure, volume, temperature, and amount, she did so in the context of cooking. She clearly tried to use her experience to explain something about the gas laws that she had read about in the textbook. However, she did not try to simplify the physical relationships she was describing by removing her kitchen context, even though that may have made it easier to describe, calculate, or match the course curriculum. The science that the students learned from Linda that day was not the science described in the chemistry textbook. Instead, it was the science that Linda learned at home. It was a little more complex than that in the book because Linda did not have an ideal system in her kitchen. It was not that the science in the book was wrong or less real than Linda's science. Both were conceptually correct; they were different because the contexts were different. Linda's story provided us with correct—not-so-correct gas law (because her interactive system prevented her from neatly labeling a constant system), and challenged how things in our class were labeled as scientifically correct or incorrect. Linda's lesson did not lead to a derivation of any of the gas laws (the relationships between pressure and volume, pressure and temperature, temperature and volume, pressure and amount), but it did lead to the derivation of some versions of the gas laws consistent with the physical qualities of gases.

What is also important to note is how this kind of conversation influenced our subsequent work on the gas laws. Later in our study of these laws, I had the students work with formal lab equipment that would provide them with opportunities to revisit their understandings of the relationships between temperature, volume, pressure, and amount in a series of controlled systems. My reasons for bringing this lab equipment to the class discussion were two-fold. First, I wanted to help students draw connections between our ideas and ideas presented by Western science, and I wanted to validate students' experiences in the context of Western science. I believed that we had created some well-formed, well-grounded, and detailed ideas about the relationships between temperature, pressure, volume, and amount by exploring how we had encountered these relationships in our past experiences (and having to talk and write about and compare these experiences). As the teacher and a chemist, I was in a position to publicly accept or reject these experiences as part of or apart from science. I was aware that the decision to involve students in rethinking the gas laws with the aid of the "formal" lab equipment might serve to devalue their own experiences. The very act of following up our ideas with verification measures—although an act synonymous with "good" scientific practice—implies that original ideas required validation and context. I believed that I might be facilitating ideas, beliefs, and actions in students that promoted the suppression of personal ideas, experiences, and voices in the name of official, non-everyday laboratory equipment and language.

Second, I was curious to learn if our own personal explorations would make our visit to "traditional science" and our participation in science less authoritarian. Would these experiences reaffirm the belief that personal experiences and understandings of the gas laws were not real science? Even if the students continued to perceive their experiences as science, would messing around with gadgets define their science for them? Would they define their own homebound work in terms of the gadgets and fancy jargon instead of redefining the gadgets and jargon in terms of their experiences? Would those students who had learned to be alienated from mechanical gadgets (as have many women, including myself) handle and explain these gadgets with confidence? These questions made me nervous, but I went ahead with the activity anyway, rationalizing my actions by telling myself over and over that I just wanted the students to draw connections between their experiences and the physical realities, formal practices and discourses of science. I addressed the group:

> Here is some equipment that we usually use in this class to present Boyle's law, Charles's law and Gay-Lussac's law.[1] I have to admit that I think these pieces of lab equipment do not do as nice a job of explaining these gas relationships as your experiences have. . . .
>   We will use these pieces of equipment to think about the gas laws as they are presented in our book, and make connections between our ideas and those ideas. Do people have questions?

The first piece of equipment (see Figure 6.1) was cold, intellectually and physically; the big shiny round metal ball that seemed to be the focal point (visually, anyway) and clearly screamed for attention had done its metallic thermal conducting duties well in the air-conditioned science building. It had been neatly packed away in the Introductory Chemistry demonstration cabinet in a tightly fitting white cardboard box. As I took the equipment out of the box, Lisa asked out loud, "What is it?" Not really knowing the best way to describe it myself, I suggested that she and any other students who wished could come up to the front table and look for themselves. Lisa, Linda, Sol, Bill, Becky, Rita, Gloria, and Holia all walked toward the front of the room while the rest of the students stayed in their seats.

The metal ball was connected to a piece of thick plastic tubing. The tubing extended into a metal handle where there was a notch, needed to let air in and out of the system. From the side of the plastic tubing extended a small balloon made of thin rubber. According to the accompanying directions to the demonstration, first, air must be pumped into the system with a bicycle pump until the balloon inflated slightly. After removing the pump and ensuring that the system is closed, one dunks the metal ball into a dry ice–acetone bath with a temperature of $-20°C$.

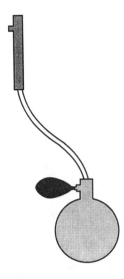

FIGURE 6.1. Apparatus with Balloon Used to Demonstrate Charles's Law

When the metal ball is submerged, the balloon deflates (see Figure 6.2) because the decrease in temperature decreases the volume in a closed system. Then the metal ball is to be removed from the dry ice–acetone bath, warmed to room temperature, and then placed in a beaker of boiling water with a temperature of 100°C. The balloon then inflates (see Figure 6.3). This demonstrates Charles's law: When temperature increases, volume increases as well.

The same equipment can be used to demonstrate Gay-Lussac's law, which relates pressure to temperature in an otherwise constant closed system. To do this, the opening to the balloon is replaced with a pressure gauge, so that the volume of the system remains constant while the pressure varies (see Figure 6.4). The same procedure is followed as with the previous demonstration except that this time observations focus on the temperature of the metal ball and the pressure gauge, rather than on the temperature of the metal ball and the size of the balloon. By immersing the metal ball in the dry ice–acetone bath (Figure 6.5), and then in the boiling water bath (Figure 6.6), one can show that the pressure decreases as the temperature decreases and that the pressure increases as the temperature increases.

We also used another piece of equipment, consisting of a square piece of transparent plastic. Embedded in this plastic was a pressure gauge with a mechanical dial. Connected to this pressure gauge was a thick piece of plastic tubing, which was connected to a syringe, also

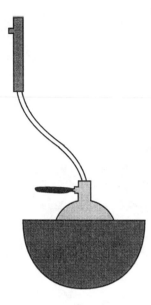

Figure 6.2. Apparatus with Balloon Submerged in Dry Ice–Acetone Bath

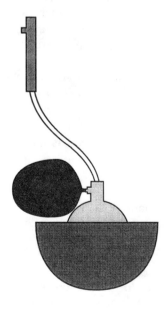

Figure 6.3. Apparatus with Balloon Submerged in Boiling-Water Bath

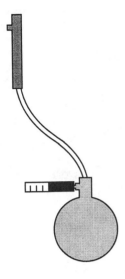

Figure 6.4. Apparatus with Pressure Gauge Used to Demonstrate Gay-Lussac's Law

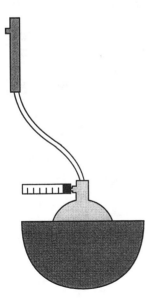

Figure 6.5. Apparatus with Pressure Gauge Submerged in Dry Ice–Acetone Bath

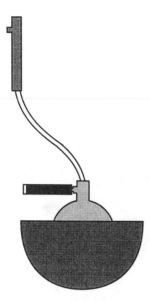

Figure 6.6. Apparatus with Pressure Gauge
Submerged in Boiling-Water Bath

embedded in the square piece of plastic. The purpose of this piece of
equipment was to illustrate that when the volume of a system increases,
the pressure decreases and when the volume of a system decreases, the
pressure increases (Boyle's law). When one changes the volume of the
system by either pushing the syringe handle in or pulling it out, the
pressure gauge indicates the change in pressure within the closed system (see Figures 6.7 and 6.8).

As the students began to pick up and muddle around with the
equipment, I stood there for what seemed like an eternity, silenced by
the implications of my own actions. Perhaps I had been right when I
had thought earlier that my choice to use this equipment was based on

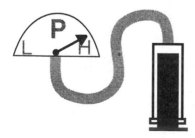

Figure 6.7. Syringe at High Pressure

Figure 6.8. Syringe at Low Pressure

my own rationalization that it was important to draw connections between "personal" and "formal" scientific discourse and practices. Perhaps I had been right that the only impact of this activity would be to redefine students' understandings of science and of the self-in-science. In the instant of that moment, I was reliving all of my interactions with a science that I learned to imitate yet be otherized from. It wasn't that we could not handle or interpret these demonstrations; it was what they represented: In all their exactness, of perfectly fitted, marked, and measured intricate little pieces, lay the foundation of a science education I hoped to challenge in my teaching practice. In a culture where we have learned to define and diminish our personal lives in the shadow of the towering institution of science, how could our personal explorations of pressure, temperature, volume, and amount in the context of everyday activities stand up to the authority of a deeply embedded institution? Despite the thousands of images and voices screaming and moving through my whole being at that moment, I could not force myself to stop the classroom activity. I could not get myself to pick up all that equipment and throw it back in the cabinet, even though that is what I really wanted to do. It was as though I was strapped into a roller coaster car already set in motion; I could not get off until the ride was over.

The students were talking among themselves about the equipment (primarily what the equipment *was*, not what it did or how it could be used to illustrate some of the relationships that we had explored earlier in the context of our lives). At the moment, I was finding the equipment rather abstract myself, even though I had used it in the past (and, admittedly, not feeling comfortable then either). For me, the demonstrations did not help me to connect with the ideas represented in the gas relationships, except in the most formal and abstract ways: I understand that the demonstrations are highly visible representations of how changes in one variable can influence the dynamics of the system, but the demonstration itself did not "speak" to any of my own personal experiences. It is rare that I ever come in contact with a metal ball that must be submerged in either boiling or freezing water. I asked if anyone wanted to help me work these demonstrations. Holia and Linda, who were already standing around the equipment, volunteered.

We began with equipment required for the Charles's law demonstration. Holia, Linda, and I worked together to set up the equipment. We borrowed Mark's bicycle pump and the college supplied everything else. After successfully setting up the needed equipment, I engaged the class in a discussion about our expectations once we immersed the metal ball in the dry ice–acetone bath:

TEACHER: This dry ice bath is very cold, about −20 or −30°C. If we submerge the metal ball in the bath, what do you think will happen to this little balloon?

BILL: The ball will decrease in temperature because the bath is cold, so the balloon will have to decrease in size.

TEACHER: Who would like to respond to Bill's idea?

[No one volunteers a response]

TEACHER: Does anybody agree or disagree with Bill?

LINDA: I think Bill's right.

TEACHER: Why?

LINDA: Well, because, like he says, Charles's law says that when the temperature decreases, the volume decreases.

TEACHER: Do you want to dunk the ball in?

HOLIA: Okay.

[The size of the balloon in fact decreases]

TEACHER: Does this remind you of any of the earlier group projects?

[The student silence here feels interminable]

TEACHER: Go back and look in your journal. What are some of the ideas we talked about earlier?

SOL: Well, nobody did this experiment, but my group talked about how you are not supposed to fill car tires with air after you have been riding on the road for a while; that's the same thing.

TEACHER: What do you mean?

SOL: Well, I guess the air is a gas and it gets warmer when the tires have been rolling against the road for a while. It makes the air expand.

TEACHER: I see your connection. Do people see Sol's connection?

[A general nodding of heads from the class]

TEACHER: Who else remembers some of the ideas we talked about earlier?

TAMMY: That one group made tea.

TEACHER: Okay, tell me more.

TAMMY: (Starting to sound nervous) Like what Sol said.

TEACHER: (Persistent) Tell me what you mean.

TAMMY: (Pleading with her friend) Kim, help.

KIM: No. (Pauses and looks at Tammy) Okay. When they heated the water for the tea, the heat made the water gas volume increase and so it came out through the teapot spout.

We continued with the rest of the demonstration. I felt very uncomfortable; I wondered if I was facilitating a return of the science that we had created to the impersonal and abstract level. Although it seemed as if my students understood the gas law relationships inherent in these demonstrations, I felt that the approach placed our personal experiences as secondary to "real science." I felt that our experiences in the kitchen and elsewhere (most of the students were women, who talked about cooking activities to explain the gas laws) were being replaced with laboratory experiences. I also think that I was more aware of those dynamics because as a woman who at home does more cooking and less of the mechanical fixing than she would like to admit, I felt a bit intimidated, or at least uncomfortable, using this abstract equipment to re-explain (to validate, as if personal experiences and theories of the world need to be validated by abstract lab equipment) my (and their) personal understandings of the gas laws. I wanted at this point to make these relationships between us in science and with science problematic with my students. I wanted somehow to begin to reposition ourselves within science.

Because I somehow felt distanced by our conversation and by the science content and process taking place, I retreated from facilitating a whole class conversation. Instead of doing the experiments with the students in front of the class, then following this with a discussion, as I had begun to do with the first piece of equipment, I changed my plan midstream. I encouraged them to work with each other in smaller groups, to play with the equipment and to explain to one another what they observed. Among the students, there was talk about what they thought they saw and any obvious gas relationships. There were questions about the equipment itself: What was it? How did it work? There was talk about nonschool-related stuff. I wonder if the nonschool talk seemed obvious to me because there were more people than there was equipment and they did not want to work in groups that were larger than normal; or if it is because they were getting bored with pressure, volume, temperature, and amount; or if they felt disconnected from these demonstrations.

After 15 minutes, I brought the class back together into a large group discussion. My intention was to talk about how the lab equipment demonstrated the formal gas relationships; I wanted to make sure that the use of the lab equipment did not remystify their understanding. I also wanted to express my discontent with my decision to use this equipment, so that if there were other students who found their experiences marginalized in science, as I had my own, by the use of the formal lab equipment, there would be a place for these feelings in class.

> TEACHER: Who wants to share an idea about the gas laws related to these experiments?
> BILL: Well, the syringe experiment shows that pressure and volume are inversely proportional.
> TEACHER: Okay, what do you mean?
> BILL: When you press the syringe in, the volume in the syringe decreases, and the pressure increases.
> TEACHER: Okay, let's hear from some other people in response to Bill or something else.
>
>   . . . .
>
> LINDA: The experiment with the metal ball wasn't that clear to me. I understand how pressure and temperature are related, but I couldn't see how the experiment worked. Can you explain it?
> TEACHER: Well, who has some thoughts related to Linda's question?
> GLORIA: This is just what I don't like about science. They always take ideas that are mostly understandable and explain them in ways which mean nothing to me. I would rather talk about popcorn than weird metal balls.
> SOL: It's true, we do not use these things every day, except maybe the syringe, so I don't think that they help that much.

After Gloria and Sol shared their ideas, many of the students nodded or vocalized their agreement. Some students were laughing, perhaps at Sol's comment about the syringe.

TEACHER: This is very interesting to me. You know, when I got out
   this demonstration equipment for you to work with, I had this
   nervous feeling. That's because I was so happy with the ways
   you described the relationships between pressure, volume,
   temperature, and amount with your own everyday experiences that I did not want to try and re-explain them with fancy
   lab equipment. So maybe I shouldn't have gotten this equipment out. Or maybe it's a good thing because this gave us a
   chance to talk about this. What do you think?
SOL: Who bought this equipment anyway?
TEACHER: The department.
[Most of the students laugh]
SOL: Can't you tell them to buy something different?
TEACHER: I think I will mention something. Let's finish talking
   about the different gas relationships; but we will go back to
   our own experiments. Juan, what do you think? Were you able
   to draw any connections between what the groups talked
   about earlier and these experiments?
JUAN: I can see how the metal ball worked, it was like filling the car
   tire with air. It does make more sense that way.

Several students echoed Juan's comment, when called on, by suggesting that the formal gas laws (Boyle's, Charles's, etc.) and the experiments performed to illustrate these laws were not very meaningful to
them. They wondered out loud why the laws were useful if they were
not realistic. We finished class that night with a discussion about the
various gas relationships, comparing how we understood them in the
contexts of our lives and with their formal presentation in Western science. In this discussion, I tried to help the students understand the
differences between the theories about gases that they had developed
earlier and those formulated in Western science. I wanted the differences to be captured through a language of ''situated knowledge''
rather than in terms of correct-incorrect. After I did this, I questioned
my decision to compare their experiences and formulations of the gas
laws with those of Western science, because it appeared that the students' ideas were perceived as secondary to Western science—as less
important than the ideas of science. Even though we had used the
complexities of our lives and hence our stories about gas laws to understand and critique the formal gas laws, I was afraid that this summing
up activity had undermined all that we had done earlier. I had tried to
emphasize the students' positional knowing of gases; this, however,
seemed to be overshadowed by correct formal science.

POSITIONING SCIENCE

In this story, the scientific knowledge developed in this class grew out of the students' interests and backgrounds, which are highly individual and culture-specific—cooking, child care, mechanical work (Barton & Osborne, 1995). Working in groups, students theorized about how they had used their knowledge or understanding of the relationships between pressure, volume, temperature, and amount in an intuitive sense at home or work. They publicly shared with one another the ways in which their own set of lived experiences had provided them with a context in which to name the gas laws, in ways different from (or, in some cases, similar to) chemistry. Central to constructing new knowledge in class about the gas law relationships was the opportunity for students to articulate their own naming of these relationships (with or without the technical jargon). The "chemistry formulation" of these ideas was situated as secondary. We used these personal explorations to develop theories consistent with and connected to our personal observations, beliefs, and values. Furthermore, we used our theorizing of the gas laws as a base from which to understand and then critique Western science. That is critical to this teaching. It is one thing to help students conceptually understand science from the standpoints of their own lives. It is quite another to help them use that personal knowledge to understand, then critique, a powerfully long-standing and excluding discipline. This starting point is important in creating a science for all Americans because it starts from the experiences of the students and uses their knowledge so they may build a science of their own and see the connections between that science and the traditional discipline.

The gas laws story also sheds some light on what it might mean to use our positionality productively to create a more liberatory science education. For example, because the study of the laws began with centering the students' gendered and cultured experiences and the complexity inherent in those experiences, the students were able to build a complex understanding of the physical world. Yet their understandings were different from those in Western science because the complexity and contradictory locations of their lives were valued in class. Before the formal lab equipment incident, I had shaped the classroom conversation in such a way that students would use their experiences to develop their own theories about the natural world rather than to validate the science prescribed. I was not seeking to categorize their experiences according to the tradition of the gas laws. I wanted to let the students' theories stand for themselves. If there was enough evidence to contradict the prescribed categories of the canonically accepted body of knowledge in science, then we would need to seize that opportunity to make explicit the divergences between such theories and to change the science in our lives.

In pushing our understanding of these discontinuities, we were faced with the implicit decision of either to silence our complexity, in acknowledgment of the authority of science; or to define and practice our lived theories, in opposition to the standpoint of science. In choosing this space of resistance—in choosing to recognize publicly that we were speaking from and about our subjectivities—we had theoretical standpoints from which to rethink and rewrite our own experiences in science. Explicitly locating these divergences, we had the chance to re-read the science in our lives and our lives in science. These spaces of radical resistance gave reasons for and contexts in which to disrupt the neatly packaged hegemonic reality in and of science. The creation of these spaces pushed against the boundaries of Western science, and as a result, as a community, we were able to begin to decenter the traditional power arrangements in science and the traditional knowledge base of science. We were able to reposition ourselves in science. Comments made by Gloria reflect this stance: "Yeah, I know what she's saying. The metal ball, it wasn't like it was part of me and I spend my days working with equipment and working with the guys, so that's not it either. It's hard to explain."

This conversation about socially and historically located interpretations of everyday events enabled the students to build a beginning knowledge critical of the identities, beliefs, and values traditionally attached to the roles we play within science class as scientists and teachers and students of science. Through our joint efforts to begin our formulation of the gas relationships from the standpoints of our lives, we began to uncover and unfold the boundaries of ideologies that structure how we think about science and ourselves in science, thereby imploding, or at least blurring, the insider/outsider dichotomies that structure and bound our relationships with and in science. When we began to formulate ideas about the pressure, volume, temperature, and amounts of gases, through exploration of our everyday experiences (not recognized as science), we had an opportunity to reflect on our lived experiences in the context of science as well as an opportunity to reflect on science in the context of our lived experiences.

I believed that much of what is oppressive in science class is a result of the power arrangements that are invoked in relationships. In our science class, the institutions of science and education played a central role in our relationships, and their centrality had defined for us not only what science was, but who we could be in science through constructing a set of dichotomies: insider/outsider, scientist/nonscientist, teacher/ student, self/other—dichotomies that clearly indicated whether we knew science and/or whether we were a part of science. Teaching this unit, however, with help from the students, helped me to see how pervasive those power arrangements were. I had thought in the past how such power arrangements, which determine what science was and who could do science, were manifested through structures such as exams, the lecture format, and fancy terminology, but I had not realized how the insider/outsider, scientist/nonscientist dichotomies were present in almost every structure in the classroom; they were certainly present in those two pieces of lab equipment. Centering the students' lived experiences so to question science helped them to reposition their understandings of and relationships with the gas laws. I do not believe that our use of examples from home and work to make sense of scientific knowledge was all that radical or liberatory, even though it provided us with a way of making sense of a set of physical properties. However, analyzing the science from that standpoint was radical. Many students in the discussions following the study of the gas laws talked about how and why they felt so apart from and so much like outsiders to chemistry. And many of these feelings connected with the students' feelings of either "being in" or "being out" of science and to the idea that chemistry renames everyday experiences in incoherent, abstract ways that are discontinuous from everyday life. This last point was brought out strongly when Gloria commented, "This is just what I don't like about science. They always take ideas that are mostly understandable and explain them in ways which mean nothing to me. I would rather talk about popcorn than weird metal balls."

When I think about the students' standing up to science through their critique of the lab equipment, I am reminded of the words of Paulo Freire (1970):

> It is only when the oppressed find the oppressor out and become involved in the organized struggle for their liberation that they begin to believe in themselves. This discovery cannot be purely intellectual but must involve action; nor can it be limited to mere activism, but must include serious reflection: only then will it be praxis. (p. 52)

The students were able to label science as the oppressor when it framed their experiences as subordinate. Although throughout the semester I had worked through several critiques of science with the students, I had not introduced that notion into our talk about the gas laws. I felt uncomfortable sharing the formal lab equipment with the students, yet

I had not even mentioned this to them. Through their theorizing about their lives and using their positional understandings to analyze science, they were able to break down the authority of science in a struggle for liberation.

Rethinking our understanding of science, as well as our relationships with science, seems critical in light of recent ethnographic work involving gender, race, and class. As is pointed out by Spender and Sarah (1980) in their ethnographic study of the girls in England, Gaskell (1992) and Connel, Ashenden, Kessler, and Dowsett (1988) in their respective studies of Canadian working-class girls and Australian students, and Patthey-Chavez (1993) in her study of Latinos in California, female, working-class and minority students may understand, at least implicitly, that schools affirm white, middle-class, male culture to the disqualification of their own views of the world. Consequently, despite the best intentions of teachers, many of these students resist the middle-class, white, male ways of schools in favor of the world of their own experience—working class, minority, female.

POLITICAL AND SOCIAL IMPLICATIONS FOR POSITIONING SCIENCE THROUGH EXPERIENCE

The story of the gas laws is a relatively unproblematic example of how the ways in which lived experience is valued in science class can influence what counts as science, because it remains, for the most part, within the confines of the classroom. But what happens when it is not as simple as lab equipment? The story of Juan's question, described in the previous chapter, had serious political and social implications for what kind of, how we talked about, and access to science in our chemistry class. Juan's experiences with medical cyclotrons were, in his mind, marked by racism and classism. Although such political dimensions to atomic theory and its applications are themselves not changed in their physical reality through the existence of classism and racism, the reasons for which they have been understood and applied, the future developments in this area of research and the ways in which Juan is able to engage them have been.

Learning about atomic theory from Juan's standpoint complicates the study of science on many levels. First, it challenges the positivistic tradition of science as a value-free endeavor. To return to the feminist critique of Western science, one of the myths of science is that it is created separate from social and cultural interests. Yet feminist scientists and philosophers of science have shown that science is subservient to these interests. Research questions and answers emerge from certain political, cultural, and socioeconomic frameworks. Juan's experiences raise serious questions about the value-free dimension of science when the study of atomic theory is merged with biochemistry. For example, as a result of medical cyclotron clinical studies, what can we learn about cancer cell growth retardation in various soft tissue cancers? Does it behave similarly in different kinds of people (taking into account race/ ethnicity, gender, lifestyle, etc.), or are generalized statements about its effectiveness being made without the use of a truly representative sample of the population? Why is it that the medical cyclotron is only a secondary application of basic cyclotron research, and what is it about what we know about particle separation and cancer cells that led researchers to test neutron beams on cancerous prostate cells?

Second, Juan's story complicates science by questioning, in addition to value-embedded research, the objectivist way of knowing in science that requires the scientist to look upon natural phenomena (including other people) as isolated objects that exist outside the context of interrelationships of which human beings are a part; that scientists describe their observations as though they and their activities exist in a vacuum (Hubbard, 1986). Juan's story calls this perspective into question by illuminating the extent to which the complexity of individuals and their intricate relationships to the world are ingredients of discovery.

Third, Juan's story complexifies science by raising questions about who has access to it. Although this particular question does not challenge the science itself, as did the other two, it does challenge the fundamental assumption that science is created to advance society. This is because Juan's story calls into question class and racial divisions in our society and whom these divisions benefit. One might argue that these kinds of arguments ought to be saved for social studies classrooms. However, from a feminist standpoint, once the objectivity of science is called into question, one cannot ignore the presence and the roots of the subjective influence. Juan's mother's being denied access to the benefits of science only raises the question of her denied access to the invention of science through formal channels.

REREADING LIVED EXPERIENCES FOR A LIBERATORY SCIENCE EDUCATION

> Making this theory is the challenge before us. For in its production lies the hope of our liberation, in its production lies the possibility for naming all our pain. (hooks, 1994, p. 75)

The Personal as Political

Within the past 5 years, there has been a growing attack on the feminist notion that the personal is political (Giroux, 1992; Mercer, 1990; Rutherford, 1990). Giroux (1992) summarizes much of this debate when he writes that "one has to now genuflect before the discourse of "authentic experience" in order to be taken seriously . . . the politics of experience is questionable on any number of grounds" (p. 312). He argues that to accept the authority of experience uncritically is to forget that identity is complex, contradictory, and multilayered. He suggests, further, that using the personal as political results in a form of "confessional politics."

Using personal experience to rethink science has been central to my efforts to construct a feminist liberatory science education and to my attempts to "research" my efforts toward those teaching goals. Although this route has caused me to share parts of my life with the reader and with my students, I do not see that as "confession." It is not an admission of doing something essentially wrong—an action, thought, or conversation that has denied social justice or social transformation for the "greater good." The personal as political—although a reminder and a source for the deconstruction of our own actions—is neither a pleading for forgiveness nor an admittance of a life of sin. Rather, it is a political declaration that our lives are holistic—that everything we do informs other things and cannot be ignored. It is a way to make clear the power, limits, and partiality that inscribe my own sense of identity in science and in education, my relationships with these institutions and the people acting within, and my own visions for change. Central to making this work is the process of viewing our experiences with a critical eye. What is the point of rethinking science from our experiences without being critical of them? Science has done this all along; it is objectivist and positivistic. The science community has successfully attempted to depoliticize cultural differences by inserting itself in a power-neutral discourse. The very act of recognizing that our experiences are embedded with social values and locations makes our efforts to rethink science inherently political and radical. For me, positionality in feminist liberatory education is about critically rereading lived experiences and interrogating science and our experiences through connections to our lives.

Breaking Down Dichotomies

The stories about the gas laws and the medical cyclotron illustrate how the science grew out of the students' lived experiences. They illustrate that because the students' experiences involved many things besides science, the science the students learned was not confined to traditional scientific concepts and principles, or even processes. In fact, I would argue, a significant piece of using lived experiences to create science is the decentering of science. Science was represented as something that was integrated in messy ways with other things. "Doing science" was part of, but not more important than, everything else that went along with the things the students did, such as family and work activities. One way to think about decentering science is to think about the "fuzzy" borders encountered and also created by the students that separate "science" from other things. Using this argument, it is easier to see how the role of science class was not simply to help the students "do science" but rather to do that which grows out of their questions and experiences. It was not to fit their experiences into science; it was to fit their questioning and critique into their experiences. This distinction is important because it blurs the borders of science in two ways. First, it removes the binary distinction from "doing science" or "not doing science" and "being in science" or "being out of science." Second, it allows connections between students' lifeworlds and science to be made more easily. This is significant because as feminist arguments remind us, much of the culture, discourse, and content of science is reflective of male, Western, and middle-class values (Harding, 1986). Using lived experiences to create and decenter science provides space for multiple voices to be heard and explored. When this happens, students learn that their experiences do not have to be channeled into defending a particular reality and that there is room for them to choose and play around with their representations of science and their identities within science.

The very act of teaching students the culture of science, or the ways of being in science, is an explicit suggestion that there are certain ways of acting and being in science that are right and certain ways that are wrong. There is no room within the routine of science to place science inside out or upside down. There is no room to explore alternatives to the power hierarchies that attempt to bound and categorize our social and physical existence. There is no room to reposition ourselves, to publicly shift the meaning of knowledge. Therefore, part of my feminist agenda in science education is to create a learning community for students where we can explore ideas about science, ways to be in science, and relationships to have in science that are continuous with and interrogative of our lived experiences. These instances are important not just because the students may have learned something about the world around them, but because both they and I learned something about our being in the world. We learned about and experienced new kinds of relationships in science, new kinds of social relationships with each other, new kinds of acting and talking in science class. Experiencing this positional way of knowing gave us space to bring new language to understanding the official and routine practices of science, a space to imagine what life could be like without the routines of science.

Gloria's talk about weird metal balls, Val's about giving birth, and Juan's about his mother are powerful instances where the routines of science were turned upside down and inside out. Not only were these students able to explore what they knew about gases or atomic theory in ways that connected to their lived experiences, but they also challenged the authority and status of science. Furthermore, it is precisely the official, or rather the mundane, when allowed to decenter science, that enabled us to turn science inside out.

The stories described in this chapter reveal the importance of revisioning and repositioning science through lived experience. By engaging in a conversation about socially and historically located interpretations of everyday events, several students were able to build a beginning knowledge critical of the identities, beliefs, and values traditionally attached to the roles we play within science class, as scientists and as teachers and students of science. Through our joint efforts to begin our formulation of the gas relationships from the standpoints of our lives, we began to uncover and unfold the boundaries of ideologies that structure how we think about science and ourselves in science, thereby imploding, or at least blurring, the insider/outsider dichotomies that structure and bound our relationships with and in science.

We also had the opportunity to speak semipublicly about the connections, contradictions, and parallels that we felt existed between our selves and the chemistry that we were in class to learn. A few students critiqued the formal presentation of the gas laws because it seemed abstract and disconnected from our own experiences and observations in the world. In other words, making connections between "scientific ideas" and our experiences—making the relationship between ourselves and science open for discussion—meant exploring assumptions we hold about ourselves, each other and science. As Linda talked about her experiences with cooking spaghetti, she began to construct new relationships with and in science. She had thought of her knowledge in the kitchen as "commonsense cooking," but by talking through those ideas and her experiences with a small group of students who shared similar experiences, she began to use her understanding of herself and her knowledge of her world to decenter the claims of a positivistic ideology in science and their place in her life, in order to allow other dynamics to shape her vision of science and her identity in that science.

The Role of Situated Knowing in Liberatory Science Teaching

I am reminded of the work of Max van Manen (1988) in phenomenological studies. He writes of modern social science research in education as separating pedagogy from the child:

> Can you find the child? Where does all this theorizing and research still connect with the lifeworlds of the children? Rather, teaching is to live our lives with children more fully; educational research so often seems to be cutting us off from the ordinary relations we adults have with children. . . . In modern forms of human science research in education, children may once again be recognizably present; however, their presence betrays a lack of pedagogic commitment to them. The children may be there as objects of our human interest in them—but they are not morally present in that they force us to reflect on how we should talk and act with them and how we should live by their side. (p. 439)

My intentions in theorizing as a teacher-researcher must include the lives of my students and myself to create in a public forum a living body of science that does not deny cultural heritage through our existence as complexly socialized and labeled people. In my own teacher-research efforts, thinking about positionality has helped me to understand that the importance of allowing our knowledge construction (scientific knowledge and critiques) to explicitly embody the complexity in our lives with and in science so that we can live and act openly and honestly in science. As Magda Lewis (1993) wrote:

> I am convinced that the struggle over pedagogy is not to fit women into the phallocentric model for social relations and work and family life, a project that will always "leave us on the short end of life" (words from a song by Arlo Guthrie). Feminist pedagogical practices are more than critique, just as they are more than making women historically and currently visible in the curriculum. . . . We can not bring about social change from within those concepts and practices that have limited our possibilities. (pp. 40, 42)

I did not want to use students' experiences to validate the prescribed science. I wanted students to use them to develop their own theories about that natural world. I was not seeking to categorize these experiences according to the tradition of the gas laws, as I had in the spring semester. The students were constructing their own knowledge about the laws, and about what is important when they study them. Their knowledge was generated, at times, in opposition to the hierarchical scientific tradition, which labeled their everyday experiences as unimportant and trivial. The students labeled their experiences with gases as important and as more complex than science could describe. The students (and I) were openly struggling against the power of the dominant culture (in science) claims to truth, to descriptions for the world. I pushed my students to be critical of the texts they were reading, because those texts denied their reality. As Chinosole, one of the professors in Maher's and Tetreault's study of feminist classroom, suggests:

> We create the knowledge, and just because our creations are not in places where knowledge is held, which is in the textbooks, that doesn't mean we didn't do it. . . . When you talk about Black women's lives from a [white] feminist perspective you really don't read about our mothers, our aunts, our sisters, all the women we know. (quoted in Maher and Tetreault, 1994, p. 65)

Chinosole describes the knowledge generated in her ethnically diverse Wild Women in Music and Literature course. This also describes some of the changes made through my own attempts at a feminist liberatory education in science. I began to see that our real critiques of science and our lives in science grew out of an articulation of positional knowing. Using students' lived experiences as locations for revisioning science does more than validate their personal experiences, although I believe that to be a very important act. Because personal experiences occur within and are reconstructed through social frameworks, students' experiences should shape the social and political dimensions of our class conversations. I can legitimate particular ideas about and experiences in science that challenge long-standing power arrangements in science and education. This kind of valuing of lived experience in science class complexifies individual and collective images of specific science content as well as of overarching visions of science. I believe that these images of science and each student's developing relationship with science are more important than "mastery" of particular scientific concepts.

Feminist literary criticism urges women to be "resisting readers" (Fetterely, 1976). I wanted my students to be resisting readers and resisting practitioners of science. I wanted them to embrace, yet distrust, the subjective knowledge of science. I wanted them to read and practice science in ways that would value personal (autobiographical) knowledge, knowledge emerging from their lives as inscribed yet agentic people rather than to let their knowledge of science rest in abstract and intellectual science. I wanted the students to "combine their subjective reactions with emerging tools of analysis, and then to form a more broad-ranging set of connections with feminism and literary theory. . . . to construct a knowledge that was useful to them" (Maher & Tetreault, 1994, p. 71).

Repositioning the Discourses:
Framing a Science for All

It is the middle of August. I am sitting in my office at Ashton preparing to turn my students' grades in to the administration. I have the last official word about which of my students knew chemistry and which did not. By the time my watch reads 5 o'clock, everything my students and I have talked, laughed, and written about, as well as resisted, will be officially reduced to a number that will be recorded in the data banks at the community college.

I am taking my time with this process even though there is not much to do. Most of the students already know their grade, because we discussed them individually. In these cases, I presented to the student my idea for a grade, and then opened our conversation to negotiation. Students have known since the beginning of the semester that they can play a role in determining their grades if they like through personal learning projects and discussions with me. I take a slow approach to grading because the very act of defining our work together through a decontextualized number, signifying academic achievement in the department's chemistry program, leaves me feeling like a disembodied abstraction, scattered in fragments across a bubble sheet scorecard.

I am also working slowly because there is an awful thunderstorm moving its way across campus. I'd rather not walk out to my car until the storm has passed. In many ways, I think that this storm is symbolic of our summer semester as well as of my teaching-researching-writing. It stormed on several class nights, so that many of my students and I would stand together by the door facing the parking lot sharing stories as we waited, slowly getting up the nerve, one by one, to walk or run out to our cars, bikes, or bus stops. Rarely did these conversations focus on chemistry.

I have always associated storms with power and uncertainty—the thunder, the lightning, the possibility for tornadoes. I also think of storms as a sort of communal reemergence of life, of possibilities. After the storm has passed, I notice the singing birds, the squirrels, and the people moving freely outdoors.

This is much of the same way that I feel about teaching and learning right now—Power, uncertainty, and possibility. I am reminded of yesterday afternoon. I spent the afternoon in office hours. We are required at Ashton to hold one office hour a week, but I usually hold more to make sure that the students have a chance to see me, if they want to, given that the students I teach have rather diverse schedules. My schedule is demanding, and so if I do not have office hours, I am typically not even on campus. This week, I also wanted to make sure that any student who has not had the chance to talk to me about her or his grade would have an added opportunity.

Late in the afternoon, Tammy came to my office. Tammy was a quiet student during the summer. I recognized her shyness immediately at the time, and as I write my stories about teaching during the summer, I am reminded of it; I hear her voice very little in the tapes I made of class—usually only when I call on her. When Tammy entered my office, I was a bit surprised because we had already discussed her grade, so I thought that perhaps she wanted her copy of her project back. She had done a really interesting piece where she created a game centered on atomic theory (I think she knew that was my favorite topic in class). She had created questions that were intended to help players think about the different pieces of atomic theory as well as the historical development of the atomic theories. What I found most interesting was that her game had no winners or losers. There were special steps built in for whole group work when an individual player could not work through an atom problem alone.

When I began to tell Tammy what I really liked about her project, she quickly thanked me and said that the real reason she came by was to thank me for the course. She then opened her backpack and pulled out a little bag, handed it to me and said she felt that for the first time she had learned something in a science class. I asked her what she learned; I do not remember her naming anything in particular except her feeling that she had not been mastered by science. After she left, I opened the bag and found a loaf of apple bread, a bag of coffee beans, and a card. The inscription on the card read, ''Thank you teacher!'' In the card, Tammy had written, ''Thank you Angie for your hard work. I hope these coffee beans help keep you awake as you try to finish your PhD. I know you will do great!''

Power, uncertainty, possibility . . . (Journal, August 9, 1994)

IMPLICATIONS OF FEMINIST TEACHER RESEARCH FOR KNOWING IN SCIENCE TEACHER EDUCATION

It is summer again. Three years have passed since I embarked on this teacher research project; 3 years of searching for ways to help create a meaningful science in the lives of my students, to bring the meaningful lives of my students into science. The students whom I write about in this book have moved onto activities other than introductory chemistry at the college, and yet their lives in that class—their learning, their writing, and their thoughts—have been abstracted as data for my project (Middleton, 1993, p. 147). With the aid of science—tape recorders, computers, transcription machines—I inscribed our voices onto disk. On the computer, I moved from file to file and cut and pasted pieces of transcripts, journals, interview notes into this chapter and that. I used my power to record and transcribe as well as my power to interact comfortably and unproblematically with science to write a story about feminism, liberatory education, and science. My teaching and research through the lens of positionality begs that we bring new ideas, concerns, and dilemmas into the science education debate. It begs that we reconsider the relationships between experience, knowledge, and power in science and the science classroom, and the implications that these relationships have for how students and teachers choose to define science and themselves in science. In what follows, I develop the following issues as potential sites in the exploration for liberatory science education: the reflexive relationships between positionality, teaching, and research in science education; schools and science as political sites for transformative praxis; reframing a knowledge base for teachers to emphasize positional and situated teaching, knowing and learning, and experience; and positioning reform in the larger discourses of power and possibility.

THE REFLEXIVE RELATIONSHIPS BETWEEN POSITIONALITY, TEACHING AND RESEARCH IN SCIENCE EDUCATION

I [engage in] feminist efforts to empower through empirical research designs which maximize a dialogic, dialectically educative encounter between researcher and researched. (Lather, 1988, p. 569)

> What I suggest is that our intent more consciously be to use our research to help participants understand and change their situations. (Lather, 1988, p. 581)

Positionality is a messy way to think about teaching science. Through this study, I have found that articulating my own position among and within various groups, the understandings that I have because of these positionings, and how these influence my relationships in science class aids the process of developing a critical awareness of own personal beliefs and values about science and education. Because examining and articulating a teaching practice through positionality is self-reflexive, it helps me, as a teacher-researcher, to continually rethink the values, knowledge, and practices that go into teaching a liberatory science.

From this perspective, then, teacher research is critical to feminist research agendas because it helps to identify and address both implicit and explicit assumptions that unproblematically guide the teaching and learning of science in schools. To come to a greater understanding of how a feminist agenda can be lived in the classroom by teachers and students, it is necessary to understand how a teacher's actions and reflections can be informed by underlying assumptions about science and school. I know that my own personal reflections on what it means to bring a feminist agenda to science education have made it obvious to me that the ways in which I act upon my own feminist teaching agenda are contextually dependent. I make sense of this agenda in connection with my understanding of myself and of the world, the understandings and experiences that my students bring to class and my interpretation of those experiences, and my beliefs about the content that I teach. This reflexive thought in teaching can move science teaching toward its liberatory potential.

For example, as I described earlier in my discussion of teaching the gas laws, teaching about the cyclotron, and even engaging in conversation with my students about their oral history projects, I feel in many ways caught between trying to help students gain access to the culture of power in science (learning traditional Western science) and inventing a new science that values their lived experiences. My feelings of being pulled in two opposing directions is not new. I knew from the beginning that I would have problems enacting my agenda while still maintaining the mission of the chemistry department. Thinking about positionality brought this tension to the surface, and it provided a language and a space in which to deal with this conflict. This tension was itself a "crossroads"—a site of multiple positions from which to rethink my science teaching and the students' science learning (Alcoff, 1988). Understanding that ambivalence becomes a "way of re-positioning our-selves" (Jacobs, 1994, p. 16), and has helped me to recognize the rea-sons for my struggle between valuing Western science or valuing my students. It was not whether I could bring a feminist critique to class, because in either case the reality of Western science is still maintained. Rather, what was important was how (and if) I made room for the students' lived experiences as a source of a science imagined in class. Could we find ways to make explicit our subjective experiences with and understandings of science in class as a multiple and shifting lens from which to reread science? For example, my agenda helps me to critique the patriarchy of science from the outside, but my privilege of being white and educated has allowed me to critique race and class from the inside. We all needed to learn about one another's subjectivities in order to deconstruct science.

This kind of reflexive relationship between articulating and critically examining positionality, teaching, and researching is a location of trans-formative praxis. By locating my research methodology as a subjective political act for social change, I am creating an evolving form of trans-formative feminist praxis. A political commitment in research to change and be changed is a form of feminist praxis, because it "encompasses both reflection and action as a form of inquiry that promotes a better, fairer, more humane world" (Miller, 1990, p. 13). For example, as a teacher, I draw on my knowledge of science, the students, and the larger social context of schooling to promote the kinds of teaching and learning that I feel is appropriate in introductory chemistry. I know certain things about my students, chemistry, education theory, feminist theory, and liberatory education. I also know that my ultimate goal is to help students build a relationship with science that does not deny their lived experiences, is critical of the ability of science to speak for people, and also interrogative of personal and communal values. Part of this relationship is knowing how to interact in and with the culture of sci-ence. This is important because one requires a knowledge of the scien-tific culture and a knowledge of the connections and divergences be-tween a "home" culture and the culture of science to interact with science.

Laurie, Tracy, and Gene, along with the rest of my students, taught me that feminist praxis is, by its very nature, evolving. Part of doing feminist praxis as a science teacher is finding ways to help all of us use our agentic positions to challenge ideas, beliefs, and relations in science that silence or oppress our lived experiences. The process of sharing stories of our lived experiences in the summer conversations and in class during the summer semester highlighted the agency we all have in changing the science in our lives. By creating opportunities in science class in which to understand how knowledge is constructed through experiences, we learned how such knowledge reflects subjectivities, and how it relates to power, privilege, and oppression. We were able to interrogate the assumptions of scientists and society. By having the chance to rearticulate and give new meaning to our experiences in the study of the gas laws, we developed a better understanding of how the power arrangements influence our relationships with and in science.

I hope that my stories show how my ideas about feminist liberatory education and about praxis have changed slowly over time through the course of teaching-researching. I believe that allowing the stories of the lives of my students to intervene in my own life, and in my teaching and research has taught me that any sort of liberatory learning setting in science requires an examination of lived experiences in science. Because our lives are our theories for science and our interactions with science, how can a feminist liberatory education (and praxis in science class) be anything but evolving? I will never know how my students' lived experiences will locate them in science or locate the science in their lives without creating a setting within to explore that issue together. I can know science as my own life has allowed me to interact with it, and I can develop a growing knowledge of how my present and past students' lives will have interacted, but these can never serve as a fundamental understanding of how my future students will interact with science. Even if they could, I am constantly changing, so my interactions with students are continually altered. For these reasons, feminist liberatory education can never be defined with certainty; it is constantly shifting.

Cochran-Smith and Lytle (1990) write that ''the voices of teachers themselves, the questions the teachers ask, the ways teachers use writing and talk in their work lives, and the interpretive frames teachers use to understand their practice'' (p. 2) are pieces that are missing from the knowledge base in education. I believe that my own engagement in teacher research will help to point out how feminist theory and practice blend together in the classroom. With the current momentum to prescribe a knowledge base for teachers, I hope that my own efforts as a teacher-researcher in the classroom will contribute to this effort in a way that is unsettling. I hope that my efforts highlight the situated and relational nature of teaching and knowledge in the classroom and how it is impossible for a teacher to know ''what you need to know'' without knowing the students and learning about their lived experiences.

I believe strongly that the educational field has much to gain from teacher research. As Cavazos (1994) points out, the voices of teachers and the voices of women are missing from science education research. Through teacher research, I hope to contribute to the research efforts to make problematic the relationships between the knower and the known, the researcher and the researched, and knowledge and authority (Lytle & Cochran-Smith, 1992). Although teacher research lends itself to these self-reflexive analyses of research, knowledge, and power, it also leads to serious questions of generalizability. If the theoretical framework brought to this sort of research is one that seeks to make sense of classroom practice in light of traditional assumptions about students and school (i.e., the uncritical and the unpolitical), then, like other forms of research, teacher research can and will contribute to the legitimization of oppressive research and teaching practices that counteract feminist agendas (Hollingsworth, 1994a). By engaging in a form of teacher research that seeks to challenge and transform traditional assumptions of students and school, I hope to not only push my own practice as a teacher towards more liberatory aims, but also to create new spaces in teacher research for nontraditional voices.

SCHOOLS AND SCIENCE AS POLITICAL SITES FOR TRANSFORMATIVE PRAXIS

The feminist position that is used in understanding science teaching at community colleges draws its strength explicitly from the ideals of education for freedom or liberatory education and implicitly from a critique of the ideals of education as schooling. Although situated within a particular physical and temporal reality that demands its own particular response, doing feminist science with community college students responds to and builds its strength from a set of the ideals about liberatory education common to all levels of science education. My purpose here is not to trivialize the uniqueness of researching the teaching of science or of any subject at the community college. Community college education is an area of teaching and research that fits under the umbrella of adult and continuing education, a field defined by its own identities, questions, and purposes. The American Association of Community and Junior Colleges (1988), Peter Jarvis (1993, 1995), and Merriam and Cunningham (1989), among others, do an excellent job of detailing the political, pedagogical, financial, curricular, and programmatic challenges of this field of research. I believe, however, that it is important to utilize the feminist standpoint developed in this book to actively link the challenges presented in community college science education to those faced by all science educators, and in particular K–12 science educators. In what follows, I utilize the challenge of education versus schooling to draw important parallels in teaching science from a feminist standpoint at the community college and K–12 levels.

It is important to situate this discussion of science education versus science schooling within the context of the purposes and goals of schooling at the various levels and their relationships to society. Historically, the goals and purposes of education have been described through two major paradigms: functionalist theories and conflict theories.[1] Functionalist theories have dominated discussion about the purposes and goals of schooling in the United States, primarily because they espouse a meritocratic belief system. They are wedded to the ideas of equalities of opportunity and access and the assumption that education promotes mobility in a fair and equal way (Bourdieu & Passeron, 1977). Furthermore, functionalist theories assert that schools are meant to assort and select students for different academic and vocational paths and that this process is important and justified because it is used for assigning labor to appropriate positions (Rubenson, 1989). Conflict theories, which serve as the backbone for critical and feminist analyses of schooling, grew out of disillusionment with the functionalist theories and their inability to adequately and fairly address the serious problem of the progressively increasing gap in scholastic achievement between particular groups of students (girls versus boys, minorities versus whites, working class versus professional class). Conflict theories contest the meritocratic nature of schooling. They position assortment and selection in schooling as a means of maintaining race, class, and gender stratification in an attempt to preserve the power structure of society. In short, conflict theories view schooling as an institutionalized way of serving the needs of those dominant in society through reinforcing social inequities, producing attitudes of acceptance of the status quo, and highlighting the economic competencies of the nation over human growth and development (Greene, 1988).

Applying this critical perspective to the purposes and goals of adult education highlights the development of adult education as a direct result of society's need to provide the adult learner with the additional education necessary to sustain the knowledge, skills, attitudes, and values necessary to unproblematic participation in society. Thus, the basic purposes of adult education can be characterized as filling the need to promote citizenship, moral education, practical curriculum, and meritocratic pedagogy (Usher, Bryant, & Johnston, 1997). In an overcredentialized and technologically advanced society, adult education, and in particular community college education, has taken on the role that the high school filled in the early and mid twentieth century. In essence, community college education began to flourish in the mid-twentieth century in order to provide the kinds of continuing education needed to offer the learner what were once considered the main goals of secondary education: Citizenship, moral education, practical curriculum, and meritocratic pedagogy. Furthermore, in his book on the making of an American high school, David Labaree (1988) describes the purposes and goals that guided the development of high school as the same as those that fostered the common school movement.

These four major goals dominate all levels of schooling. Although they play out in different forms, the intention is universal: to maintain society. From a feminist standpoint informed through conflict theories, maintaining society is a dangerous thing. Whether it is a group of first graders lining up silently after recess to march to their classroom, or eighth graders learning about the success of the great American experiment of democracy, or community college students solving Boyle's law problem sets, schooling is at once about regulation, compliance, and serving (but not changing) society. Adult schooling, like primary and secondary schooling, is based on the cultural goals of perpetuating the values and morals of the dominant in society and on the social goals of reproducing those relationships in society that contribute to a market economy (Freire, 1970; Giroux, 1985). This kind of thinking has even partly informed the otherwise progressive reform initiatives in science education. Despite calls for "science for all," to promote "authentic experiences" and "student-centered inquiry," the proposed national standards and benchmarks continue to tell us that students ought to have opportunities to study science in order to increase their economic productivity and to help the United States maintain its technological and economic prowess (AAAS, 1989; NRC, 1996). Schooling community college students, or any students, in science or any other subject is about creating people who will easily and unproblematically fill the needs of society.

John Dewey (1916, 1938, 1949), in his lifework, highlighted the distinction between schooling and education. In *Experience and Education*, Dewey critically describes schooling as a site where students are "processed" by the teachers. This processing is made possible through schedules, schemes of classification, exams, promotion to new classes, and set rules and regulations for movement and action; all this to provide students with "an education." And despite the fact that the physical manifestations of these processes differ in the various countries, states, districts, school levels, and even individual classrooms, schooling remains a process in which subject matter is transmitted and sometimes imposed by the teachers onto the students. Embedded within the transmission of subject matter is a preparation for citizenship through an imposed vision of the future, a set of adult standards and values, and moral training, as defined outside of school by the dominant in society. Freire (1970), an adult educator himself, has described this kind of schooling—regardless of the age of the learner—as static; as a form of banking education where knowledge, values, and ideals are deposited in the minds of learners and where students are expected to unproblematically and passively accept these things as taken for granted. Thus stated, schooling, regardless of the level of the learner or of the physical or temporal structures that shape the school day, is often about passive immersion in the outside world and an uncritical acceptance of the taken for granted. Clearly, these progressive and critical analyses of schooling underscore the ways in which the institution of schooling has been used to maintain society.

Education, in contrast to schooling, is a dynamic process linking experience and freedom to human growth (Dewey, 1938). This contrast is important. Whereas the goal of schooling is the transmission of skill and fact, the purposes of education are the growth and maturity of the student through experience and understanding. Education shifts the emphasis from *what* is to be taught and why, to *who* is learning and why.

Freire (1970) utilizes the vision of education as a process of actively engaging participants in the wider world with his theoretical and practical study of adult literacy education. In his work, Freire illustrated how important it is for education to challenge participants to engage ideas, culture, and values critically in order to promote critical consciousness and freedom from the dehumanizing structures and the cultures of colonizers that promote oppression. Education is about a dialogic process incorporating experience and reflection, rather than the transmission of a correct set of knowledge and values. Education is a political act in which learners are provided with opportunities to process and critically reflect and act upon experience in ways that may or may not meet the needs of the dominant in society. Education is about critically examining and engaging in society rather than about maintaining it as it is.

bell hooks (1990) develops the idea of education for freedom through the questions of choice and location. "Within complex and ever-shifting realms of power relations, do we position ourselves on the side of colonizing mentality? Or do we continue to stand in political resistance with the oppressed, ready to offer our ways of seeing and theorizing, of making culture, towards that revolutionary effort which seeks to create space where there is unlimited access to the pleasure and power of knowing, where transformation is possible? This choice is crucial" (p. 145).

Education for freedom, or liberatory education, and the realities of choice and location as defined by people like Freire and hooks underscore both the uniqueness of science education at the community college and its similarity to science education at the K–12 level. To make this point more clearly, I return first to the uniqueness of the community college in the broader landscape of education for freedom. The community college is often considered the bridge between high school general education and the more specialized knowledge and rigorous work of various professional schools or colleges. It is supposed to serve as an extra bit of support that some students may need to develop confidence in their academic abilities or to develop skills in particular areas needed for further study.

I have found this notion of the bridging course to be highly problematic in my own interactions at the community college, primarily because the science department bases its authority on the intellectual tradition of science. That is, I see the science department at Ashton as practicing and promoting the long-held view of science as an intellectually demanding discipline in which only the best and the brightest can succeed. This rings true in the history of Introductory Chemistry, which I taught and which has a tradition of high drop-out rates, low average scores, and a focus on abstract, decontextualized knowing. All of this seems rather ironic given its mission as a bridging course.

In many ways, Ashton would be better described as a holding place where students wait to get the okay to move on. Students at community college are waiting to get the word, the validated certificate, that allows them to move on and up. The structure of the chemistry course that I taught—a prescribed knowledge base to learn, a prescribed set of exams that define the degree of mastery of that knowledge base, a goal of 70% as the average achievement in the course, a high drop-out rate, the lack of room for teachers to shape the course to their students (unless they do so problematically in the eyes of the department)—clearly defines the qualities needed to cross the bridge. The most obvious quality needed for successful crossing is conformity to the routine of school and science.

An important question is then raised for those who seek a feminist education in schools: Will the students who have learned to construct a relationship with science that decentralizes the authority of science contribute to their own oppression because they refuse to conform in science? Will they as a result not receive the appropriate credentials? I do not believe that this is the case. During one of our summer conversations, Gene stated that in science and education "there is both igno-rance and intelligence." His statement unsettles the debate around the purpose of teaching science to children and adults in school. To move science education beyond schooling in science also means to move be-yond the transmission of a taken-for-granted knowledge base in science and set of values and beliefs about how that knowledge was con-structed. Schooling in science, where knowledge, values, and ideals are deposited in the minds of learners and where students are expected to unproblematically and passively accept these things as taken for granted is knowledge through ignorance, regardless of the age or level of the learner. In other words, a science education that focuses on the transfer of skills and facts, and on preparing students for the workforce, ab-stracts it from the challenges of developing a "critically conscious, so-cially responsible and politically active student body and citizenry" (Leistyna & Woodrum, 1996, p. 4).

Yet this analysis meant to highlight the uniqueness of science edu-cation at the community college also uncovers the challenges of science educators across all levels: to make science education something other than a mere stepping-stone to the next level of scholastic or vocational science and to make science education something other than an act of compliance. Schooling in science—at all levels—is marked by a science education that is driven by science and mastery of a wide range of content facts rather than by the students and their explanations, inquir-ies, and lifeworlds. Even those involved in current reform initiatives in science education admit that as a community we must move beyond the ideals of schooling and rote memorization to the ideals of education and inquiry-based learning, which will provide students with the skills, knowledge, and language to engage in public debate and to make per-sonal decisions (AAAS, 1989; NRC, 1996). The feminist perspective de-veloped in this book pushes these national goals one step further through my insistence that as a community we also need to consider the ways in which such knowledge and skills have been socially and historically constructed and enacted so that they are not used by stu-dents without regard for their personal and political ramifications. This framework shifts from a science-driven education, where science is un-problematically imposed from the outside, to a student-driven educa-tion, where science and the self-in-science are continually and simulta-neously examined, challenged, and articulated.

I am reminded of Patti Lather's (1991) reflections on the work of Lentricchia, when she writes that "Lentricchia's pedagogical strategy uses deconstruction to help students create subject positions such as a kind of new person who's not going to be satisfied with the usual canonical things'' (p. 122). I believe that education in science is important only in that it teaches students how to (de)constructively deal with the science in their lives intellectually and politically. Education in science has traditionally pushed students and teachers into totalizing categories. If an education in science values the multiple and contradictory sites from which teachers and students engage one another as well as science in the material and intellectual space of science class, then the class can be viewed as a fluid social setting requiring, but also promoting, changing agentic selves (Lather, 1991).

As Lather, Dewey, Freire, hooks, and others all point out, the ideals of a liberatory education cut across subject matter, age, gender, social class, race, ethnicity, and other categories because of the ways in which the values of society are imposed upon life in schools. Schooling and science are pervasive forces in this society. They play significant roles in shaping society's view of valid research methodology and valuable knowledge. They also shape our physical lives through transportation, communication, nutrition, and health. It is not my hope that all people choose a ''career'' in science, or even that any of my students do so. It is my hope that our science does not dampen any person's agency to work for social justice or anyone's ability to imagine a world without social power hierarchies. My intention as a feminist teacher working for liberatory science education is to value students; to value their age, gender, social class, race, or ethnicity; and to create spaces where their lived experiences, their hopes, dreams and fantasies, are part of their exploration of the world and its mysteries—including, but not limited to, science.

REFRAMING A KNOWLEDGE BASE FOR TEACHERS: POSITIONAL AND SITUATED TEACHING, KNOWING AND LEARNING, AND EXPERIENCE

If science education is to encompass the question of science for all in its most inclusive sense, new questions about a knowledge base for science teachers must be addressed. For example, in what ways can a teacher's understanding of the positional nature of knowledge, identity, and power in her science classroom help her to engage her students in science? Is it possible to create a setting for science teaching and learning where the traditional paradigm of science at the center, as a target to be reached by students at the margins, shifts to one of inclusion, where students' experiences and identities remain a central focus that guides pedagogical democratic principles and that is transformed so that it becomes an integral part of their lives? Although I believe that my story illustrates this kind of teacher knowledge and that this kind of community for science teaching and learning is possible, it also illustrates that it is very difficult and that it is situated. It is difficult because it sets in motion explorations into the positional nature of knowing and being known in science and science class. This is no easy task because the positional nature of knowing and being known changes and shifts with each new group of students and as each class develops across the school year. It also calls into question the historically accepted modernist frameworks of positivism, instrumental reason, universal knowledge, and bureaucratic control that have been at the center of curriculum and practice in science education (Stanley & Brickhouse, 1995). In the case of my own science teaching at the community college, science education could no longer hide behind the modernist claim to objectivity and universal knowledge. Rather, as questions of positionality became central to science for all, it became relocated within a subjective discourse of human agency that was focused on self- and collective empowerment. Finally, it redefines science teaching and learning as a cultural practice that is accountable ethically and politically for the stories that it produces, and for the images of the past, present, and future that it deems legitimate (Eisenhart, Finkel, & Marion, 1996; Giroux, 1991; Kincheloe, 1993; WISE, 1996). In the case of my teaching at the community college, I needed to value a science that emerged from the intersections between the students'—the mothers', the chrome plate workers', the secretaries', the full-time students'—ways of knowing their world and of knowing and doing science. Because the students' experiences occurred within and were reconstructed through social frameworks, their experiences shaped the science class, from questions about access to science to proper methods for childbirth. This kind of valuing of lived experience complexifies individual and collective representations of and identities in science because it embodies the positional nature of knowledge and knowing.

Another critical piece of this knowledge base is an understanding of the situated nature of teaching. Central to this task is understanding how these relationships require the teacher to continually rearticulate her epistemological and political agendas. As I learned more about how my students and I had constructed ideas about science through exploring lived experiences in class, it became necessary that we use our lived experiences as places from which to critique and revision science and our relationships with it. Previous to these experiences with my students, my political intent was to use feminist theory, in the abstract, as our theoretical foundation. I can see now how this approach can be equally alienating, especially when many of the feminist critiques of science have emerged from a white, middle-class, academic, female perspective. In our class we were not all white, middle-class academics: The students were primarily working class, culturally diverse, and very much on the fringe of the educational process. The differences from which we began to reread the science in our lives allowed a much richer vision of science as well as the possibilities for new relationships.

The stories of the students from this particular community college illustrate the situatedness of science teaching by identifying how significantly different life experiences shape the ways in which students engage each other and the ways they think about science. They do not enter school science with an empty bag, waiting for it to be filled with interesting facts and figures. They come to school with bags already filled—with a set of struggles, sometimes reflected in the typical science curriculum, sometimes not. And if we believe, as I have argued, that knowledge, identities, and power are positional in the science classroom (and outside it), then finding ways to understand the relationships between the study of the natural world and what students already bring to school is a significant aspect of science education.

For example, as we shared our lived experiences and ideas about gases, we pushed at the boundaries of what was acceptable in science; we created new ideas about science and new relationships with and in science. We talked about things that we do in our lives that are not traditionally valued in science. Valuing lived experiences, created spaces for the resituating of relationships with science—the positivistic ideology of science in some cases was displaced as our experiences became valid and valuable parts of science education. By recognizing the moving nature of our relationships, we could begin to articulate the changes in the ways we perceive ourselves and each other and in science. Our knowledges about self and science became resituated; having an awareness of the positionality that we bring to relationships, we also had a better understanding of the power arrangements involved in such relationships. These events have helped me as a teacher-researcher to see that positionality is more than being white, being female, being a teacher, being a student, being a scientist, although these identities play central roles in the ways in which I choose to make sense of events. But these identities do not change as a result of relationships (I am still white, female, a teacher, a student, a scientist). What changes are the ways in which I understand how these identities are bounded by particular power arrangements in science and in education, and the effects of these power relations, namely, the dualisms. It is through such changes that students and teachers can reposition themselves in science and education.

Additionally, this kind of knowledge base for teachers creating a science for all requires that teaching and learning be recognized as pedagogical and political (Brady, 1995; Freire, 1970; WISE, 1996). For example, the summer conversations with Gene, Tracy, and Laurie about cancer rates, nutrition, and sexism through the context of their lived experiences was an attempt on my part to begin to understand and value the experiences and knowledge that my students bring to science class and that reflects their complex and multiple lives. It was an attempt on my part to invite into the science conversation ideas, values, beliefs, and qualities traditionally considered nonscientific, unimportant in science, to understand how these standpoints can transform science in and out of the classroom. The intention was to push at the boundaries of how valued knowledge and habits of mind are defined, to redefine science and who you must be to do science. Tracy and Gene talked about the political nature of science education and how we are all a part of "power relationships." They also talked about how these circumstances have an enormous impact on what we do in our science classes. Being able to articulate how we are all so caught up in such power relationships are a reminder of how teachers and students are defined in terms of these relationships—as teachers and students, scientists and nonscientists, men and women. It is also a reminder of how these definitions impact the ways in which students and teachers think they can talk and be inside and outside of chemistry class.

Any knowledge base for science teachers meant to promote a science for all is therefore itself situated within the reflexive relationships between self, science, schools, power, knowledge, and the social, political, and historical dimensions of experience. The students discussed here have shown us how to create a science for all—both in school and out. This kind of science for all happens when students and teacher struggle to understand and critique how their own individual and collective social and historical locations shape their relationships with each other, science, education, and society. Tracy's insight into our actions during the spring semester and the connections she drew to her personal life indicate how valuing experiences pushed against these power relationships. I had to find additional ways to allow the students to shape our class and the science in it through their wants, needs, and beliefs. Tracy's and Gene's ideas about who holds knowledge in science and society suggest that a feminist agenda goes beyond pushing the boundaries of power relationships in class to helping students become aware of the power relationships in science as well.

To create a setting for science teaching and learning that promotes doing science in a liberatory way, I asked my students to rethink their visions of school science—of Western science—and to articulate their questions and needs for science. I asked them to see that their questions came from their personal and lived theories of acting and interacting in the world. By exploring science this way, many students had a space to explore how their ideas compared to the acceptable theories promoted by the institution of science and those who work to uphold its traditions (scientists, teachers, etc.). Many students' ideas differed from those in Western science, and many saw their own ideas reinforced by Western science. I asked the students to value their own questions, arising from their current life situations, rather than to rely on answers to generic science questions from other experts' investigations. Because this approach was different from many of their usual experiences of science or school, I asked them to deconstruct, readjust, and clarify their sense of education, of science and of self in learning and living science (Greene, 1988; Hollingsworth, 1994b, p. 200; Lather, 1991).

POSITIONING REFORM IN THE LARGER DISCOURSES
OF POWER AND POSSIBILITY

As I recognized through listening to and trying to value students' lived experiences, my students are positioned differently from how I am in science and education. This situation poses a dilemma for the feminist teacher who wants to use students' lived experiences as a basis for science education. In teaching the gas laws, I encouraged the students to construct their own science about gases through their experiences and then to use these experiences to interrogate the acceptable science and their relationships with that science. As the teacher, I allowed the students' lived experiences to be the curriculum in our learning of the gas laws. However, I also recognize that not all students' lived experiences were equally valued or legitimized in our class. There were several competing factors and power arrangements that ensured that this was the case. When I teach chemistry, I impose my feminist values and political agenda on my students and on their learning. The values I enacted through my agenda were formed from my own lived experiences and reflect my interactions with a variety of often competing groups. In other words, the knowledge that I, as a white academic feminist and a chemistry teacher, bring to making sense of what goes on in the classroom is often full of contradictions because I have been socialized to view the world as white woman, scientist, student, teacher, feminist. My personal values often come into conflict with one another (such as wanting to help students see the beauty and the horror in science) or come into conflict with students who come from different backgrounds and histories (such as the conflict inherent in valuing a student's idea that may be oppressive to me or other members of the class). Not only do these conflicts exist because I impose my agenda on the students and because the department imposes its agenda on all of us, but also because the students impose their values and agendas on one another and on me. What I think is important in science class is sometimes in conflict with what the students assume is important or want to make important. The students and I interact within inscribed roles and relationships (Luke & Gore, 1992). Finally, there are the values with which science has been imbued and the values promoted by the society in which all of this takes place.

This brings to the center once again the idea of science for all, how conflicted this *all* is, and how deeply entrenched meritocratic visions of science are in schools. A science for all requires that science be changed so to be open to the multiple experiences that *all* bring. For me, teaching a science for all has in part come to mean that it is important to create spaces within which students' lived experiences can be articulated with and against the science that is accepted by society. Creating spaces for students' lived experiences helped me in my search for ways to uncover the grand narratives that structure learning in science class. It has also helped me to reflect on how feminist theories can help both my students and me to create a setting for science teaching and learning that seeks to help us understand, critique, and revision science, and our relationships with science, from our multiple and lived perspectives, and to create a science education that invites and supports diverse experiences and participation in science, in an effort to inform the goal of "science for all Americans."

In the first chapter, I wrote that I often felt alienated from science because the science that I was supposed to learn did not always connect with my experiences and intuitions about the world. I felt intimidated by a culture and a content that did not adequately connect with my experience, and I felt that I did not have the knowledge base, the language, or the confidence to challenge either science or my feelings. Yet I also wrote that by probing into the nature of science and critiques of science, I began to draw connections between some of my feelings toward and beliefs about science. Feminist critiques of science opened up new imaginings about science. I began to understand that it was legitimate to have feelings in science, that to suceed, I did not have to be able to separate myself from my object of study. I learned to characterize and make explicit the values embedded in my own scientific theorizing and to learn that scientific knowledge, by its very nature, was made stronger, more objective, through such explications (Harding, 1991). I felt liberated from feelings of intellectual deficiency and fraud (MacIntosh, 1980).

Throughout my teacher research study, I tried to create situations where my chemistry students could experience a similar kind of liberation. Of course I knew that theirs would not be the same liberation as I had experienced, because each of us brings different life stories to the study of chemistry. But I believed that there would be common elements. Through the process of exploring this teaching struggle, from a feminist perspective and through the lens of positionality, I learned that to engage students in an understanding of science that did not assume a particular cultural framework meant taking seriously the lived experiences of students. It meant allowing those lived experiences to shape and form the science and the critiques of the science that we do in class.

Through sharing with me their lived experiences in and out of science, my students helped me to interrogate how my own positionality as a feminist teacher had originally shaped my intent for a liberatory science class. My students' intervention helped me to recognize that our lives are our theories for science—that we can reread our lived experiences to create liberatory science education.

LOOKING AHEAD

For me, in many ways, the material in this book reflects the complexity of feminist work in the 1990s in the United States. There are many interconnected, overlapping, disjointed, parallel, and contradictory pieces. Traditionally, writing research takes place within a specified format. There are allocated spaces for the literature review, methodology, data, and conclusions. It is supposed to be very "scientific": The researcher goes out and "discovers" some set of Truths for the education community to use in its pursuit of knowledge. The researcher is an expert in a particular area and holds valued knowledge of something new and unique. This notion is modeled after the positivist theoretical framework traditionally used in science. Scientists "discover" knowledge that is useful and meaningful. Educating others in science traditionally follows the same ideology: Teach students the knowledge of science.

My convictions, borne out of my lived experiences and interactions with others, tell me that at no level—scientific research and writing, educational research and writing, or teaching—is objectivity possible and that there is no method that can guarantee certainty or generalizability. At every level, our knowledge and our relationships with knowledge and others is contextually dependent. Making meaning out of contextual artifacts requires a constant rereading and an understanding of the multiple locations in which any interaction occurs.

I am reminded of how Sam Hollingsworth (1994b) writes about teachers and teacher action research and how an important piece of such a practice is to critically reread our own assumptions and attitudes about education, because "such attitudes also influence the epistemological philosophies that we adapt to frame our teaching" (p. 200).

My lived experiences have brought me to this point in my thinking. Science itself has not been a source of freedom in my life, but understanding my own role in constructing and engaging that science has been liberatory. My students have clarified this point for me. As DeShawn wrote in her journal several weeks after the conversation about Martha Ballard:

> Science is more than learning about concepts and traditional scientists and that is why I think that witches and wizards ought to be included in science, although I don't agree with those terms you used. Personally, I have always thought of science as very abstract. It had little to nothing to do with what goes on in everyday life. I believe that has a lot to do with how it was taught to me. The oral report about midwives I found very interesting. I guess it changed my way of thinking as far as not see it as being absolute, but a political and economically controlled endeavor. I never read about midwives in school as far as science was concerned, or any women for that fact. It showed me history has to do with science and still does today. Whoever has the power gets the credit. Just like in every other field such as literature, mathematics or history, . . . women had to learn by trial and error and weren't allowed in school. What we really know about science is controlled, and we are given what status quo wants us to know. I guess I feel that science is like many other areas that need desperate growth before they can truly be effective.

And as Gene said during a summer conversation:

> Part of the reasons that science has emotional and ethical sides is that it is a human practice, it has a human side. For example, the

oral report by the medical intern presented last week showed me how really important chemistry is in the medical profession. Somehow I didn't realize that everything you did in hospitals required chemistry of all sorts to function, serve and cure and heal humanity. People do science and people use science. It is human. I felt it was just books, methods in education and industry, but now I realize it can come alive and influence our survival as humans. Furthermore, the injustice that women shared in the science and chemistry professions at all levels. That those men who share the elitist attitude are missing the point of science of the masses to appreciate. It is all our responsibility to change it.

The relationships that we have in science are messy, complex, and most important, alive. If as teachers and researchers we value that complexity with students in self-reflexive and active ways, then we can begin to create and enact a revisioned science. As Gene said, "It is all our responsibility to change it." I conclude with my own reflections on that responsibility:

Right now I am high above the Pacific Ocean. It is dark out, as it has been since my plane left Auckland over 6 hours ago. I am not sure what time it is where I am, but I do know that it is 1:08 a.m. Thursday morning, June 1, at the airport in Auckland from where I departed, and it is 6:08 a.m. Wednesday morning, May 31, at the airport in Los Angeles, to which this plane is headed. This isn't my favorite or my usual place to write. As a matter of fact, this is only the second time I have flown over the Pacific Ocean—the first was last week on my way to New Zealand (Aotearoa).

I have to write this journal by hand and type it into my computer later because the batteries to my laptop ran out long ago. They are supposed to last 2 hours each, but they conked out after only 40 minutes. I think that the change in voltage between my home country and New Zealand might have been the cause. Then again, maybe it is the spirits that lurk above the earth. We just hit some turbulence, the pilot says. Maybe the spirits quivered when I invoked their names.

I write this journal entry because I have been thinking about Rose, whom I met on my trip to Christchurch, a small city on Aotearoa's southern island. Rose is a vibrant Maori woman who, as an educator, teacher, researcher, and community activist, draws heavily from feminist theories and native Maori writings to find ways to bring Maori voice and customs back into New Zealand education. Rose tells me that Maori people came to the islands of Aotearoa (New Zealand) many years ago. They are the "indigenous people" of the island. The Maori, as were the 500 tribes of North America, were dominated—colonized and missionized—by English settlers several hundred years ago. Since that time, the Maori have worked hard to keep their cultural heritage. As Rose tells me, much of the Maori oral culture has been lost over the last 3 centuries as the settlers have engaged in a successful campaign of cultural assimilation.

Rose also told me that the Maori have their own system for explaining their world based on their own observations. The "ways of knowing" the Maori bring to the world are different from those of Western science. For example, they strive to always look at the whole. This is evident in the Maori medical practice, where there is no word for health or healing, but only one word, the meaning of which extends beyond health and healing to include the material existence of the person. She told me this story because she said she was very much interested in my work. She said she was interested not only because it could create spaces for the white Pakaha way to be decentralized in the Western schools that Maori children often attend, but also because the process of sharing lived experiences in a critical and supportive community allows the participants to re-read their own ideas about science.

To me, Rose expressed the power, uncertainty, and possibility in liberatory science education. Rose's comments remind me of the power and authority that I have as a white academic feminist, teacher, and researcher to choose which lived experiences in my class to value, as well as to tell others that they ought to incorporate their own and their students' life histories into their courses so that "the everyday world" and positional knowing becomes problematic (Smith, 1987). Her comments remind me of the uncertainty in revisioning science. It will never be discovered, never be complete, but always partial and changing as we work to make our understanding of the world more inclusive of multiple ways of knowing and being. Finally, her comments speak to the possibility for liberatory education in science. I do not claim to have worked through the layers of hegemonic practices that guide my teaching-researching. Yet, I know that critically rereading my understanding of science and science teaching through the lives of my students has helped me to begin to picture a science education that I had never considered possible. Rose's stories of the Maori spoke to how much more we all need to learn about Western culture, about

oppression and colonization, and about the politics of inclusiveness.

The sun is starting to rise ahead of the plane. It is now 3:00
a.m. in Aotearoa, 8:00 a.m. in Los Angeles. My muscles feel
cramped from riding in this crowded plane, but I refuse to feel
trapped. There is much work to be done in the politics of decoloni-
zation of my own mindbody and of science education. (Journal,
May 31–June 1, 1995)

Notes

All names used in this book are pseudonyms.

CHAPTER 4

1. This phrase was suggested by members of my dissertation writing group (Kathy Roth, Elaine Howes, Kathy Peasley, and Constanza Hazelwood).

CHAPTER 5

1. Each student was required to carry out a series of conversations with a local community member about the latter's views of science. These community members did not need to be scientists. Some students were allowed to read articles or books about a person to discern their ideas about science instead of interviewing a community member if they felt uncomfortable with the task or if other constraints did not permit them to engage in the activity.

2. Ann based her oral history on an excerpt from *A Midwife's Tale: The Life of Martha Ballard, Based on Her Diary 1785–1812*, by L. T. Ulrich, 1990, New York: Vintage Books.

3. In this conversation, I periodically called on people to talk; students were raising their hands, waiting. To bring some continuity to the transcript of this conversation, I have deleted the brief comments that I made, such as "Okay, Val."

4. Val often spoke freely about God in our class.

CHAPTER 6

1. As a class, we had not formally talked about these laws before. I used the names of these laws because, at that point, I intended to use the demonstration equipment to draw connections between the students' understandings of thermodynamics and Western science. I knew that many of the students were

familiar with these names because I had noticed that some students had been looking through the chapter on gas laws while they were working in groups during the previous class meeting.

CHAPTER 7

1. Goals and purposes of education are a complex subject that to be treated fairly require more than the brief description I provide here. Please refer to Bowles and Gintis (1976) and Hurn (1985).

References

Alcoff, L. (1988). Cultural feminism versus post-structuralism: The identity crisis in feminist theory. *Signs, 13*(3), 405–436.

American Association for the Advancement of Science. (1989). *Science for all Americans*. Washington, DC: American Association for the Advancement of Science Press.

American Association for the Advancement of Science. (1993). *Benchmarks for scientific literacy*. New York: Oxford University Press.

American Association of Community and Junior Colleges. (1988). *Building communities: A vision for a new century*. Washington, DC: The American Association of Community and Junior Colleges.

Amos, V., & Parmar, P. (1981). Resistances and responses: The experiences of black girls in Britain. In A. McRobbie & T. McCabe (Eds.), *Feminism for girls*. London: Routledge & Kegan Paul.

Anderson, C. W. (1991). Policy implications of research on science teaching and teachers' knowledge. In M. M. Kennedy (Ed.), *Teaching academic subjects to diverse learners* (pp. 5–30). New York: Teachers College Press.

Anyon, J. (1984). Intersections of gender and class: Accommodations and resistance by working-class and affluent females to contradictory sex role ideologies. *Journal of Education, 166*(1), 25–48.

Apple, M. (1979). *Ideology and Curriculum*. London: Routledge & Kegan Paul.

Apple, M. (1992). The text and cultural politics. *Educational Researcher, 21*(7), 4–11.

Apple, M. (1994). *Official knowledge: Democratic education in a conservative age*. New York: Routledge.

Atwater, M. (1996). Social constructivism: Infusion into the multicultural science education research agenda. *Journal of Research in Science Teaching, 33*(8), 821–838.

Barton, A. C. (1995). Developing students' ideas about chemistry through "oral histories." *Chemistry & Industry, 2*, 60.

Barton, A. C. (1996). *Politicizing lived experience in science class*. Paper presented at the annual meeting of the American Educational Research Association, New York City.

Barton, A. C. (1997a). Birthdays, alcohol, and educating homeless children. *Taboo: Journal of culture and education*. In press.

Barton, A. C. (1997b). Liberatory science education: Weaving connections between feminist theory and science education. *Curriculum Inquiry, 27*(2), 141–164.

Barton, A. C., & Osborne, M. D. (1995). Science for all Americans? Science Education Reform and Mexican-Americans. *The High School Journal, 78*(4), 244–252.

Belenky, M. F., Clinchy, B. M., Goldberger, N. R., & Tarule, J. M. (1986). *Women's ways of knowing: The development of self, voice and mind.* New York: Basic Books.

Bleier, R. (1986). *Feminist approaches to science.* New York: Pergamon Press.

Bourdieu, P., & Passeron, J. (1977). *Reproduction in education, society and culture.* Beverly Hills: Sage.

Bowles, S., & Gintis, H. (1976). *Schooling in capitalist America: Educational reform and the contradictions of economic life.* New York: Basic Books.

Brady, J. (1995). *Schooling young children: A feminist pedagogy for liberatory learning.* New York: SUNY Press.

Brickhouse, N. (1994). Bringing in the outsiders: Reshaping the sciences of the future. *Curriculum Studies, 26*(4), 401–416.

Britzman, D. (1991). *Practice makes practice.* Albany, NY: SUNY Press.

Carr, W., & Kemmis, S. (1989). *Becoming critical: Education, knowledge and action research.* London: Falmer Press.

Cavazos, L. (1994). *Women science teachers' voices.* Unpublished doctoral dissertation, Michigan State University.

Cobern, W. (1996). Worldview theory and conceptual change in science education. *Science education, 80*(5), 579–610.

Cochran-Smith, M., & Lytle, S. (1990). Research on teaching and teacher research: The issues that divide. *Educational Researcher.*

Connel, R., Ashenden, R. J., Kessler, S., & Dowsett, G. (1988). *Making the difference: Schools, families and social division.* Sydney, Australia: Allen and Unwin.

Davidson, A. L. (1994). Border curricula and the construction of identity: Implications for multicultural theorists. *Qualitative Studies in Education, 7*(4), 335–349.

Davies, B. (1989). *Frogs and snails and feminist tales.* Sydney, Australia: Allen and Unwin.

Delpit, L. D. (1988). The silenced dialogue: Power and pedagogy in educating other people's children. *Harvard Educational Review, 58*(3), 280–298.

Dewey, J. (1916). *Education and democracy.* New York: Free Press.

Dewey, J. (1938). *Experience and education.* London: Macmillan.

Dewey, J. (1949). *The school and society.* Chicago: University of Chicago Press.

Edwards, D., & Mercer, N. (1987). *Common knowledge: The development of understanding in the classroom.* London: Methuen.

Eisenhart, M., Finkel, E., & Marion, S. (1996). Creating the conditions for scientific literacy: A re-examination. *American Educational Research Journal, 33*(2), 261–295.

Fetterely, J. (1976). *The resisting reader: A feminist approach to American fiction.* Bloomington: Indiana University Press.

Feyerabend, P. (1988). How to defend society against science. In E. Klemke, R. Hollinger, & D. Kline (Eds.), *Philosophy of science* (pp. 34–44). New York: Prometheus Books.

Foucault, M. (1980). *Michel Foucault, Power/knowledge: Selected interviews and other writings 1972–1977.* (C. Gordon, L. Marshall, J. Mephan, & K. Soper, Eds. and Trans.). New York: Pantheon Books.

Fox Keller, Evelyn (1985). *Reflections on gender and science.* New Haven: Yale University Press.

Freire, P. (1970). *Pedagogy of the oppressed.* (Myra Bergman Ramos, Trans.). New York: Continuum.

Gaskell, J. (1992). *Gender matters from school to work.* London: Open Press.

Gergen, K. J. (1991). Social understanding and the ascription of the self. In J. W. Stigler, R. A. Shweder, & G. Herdt (Eds.), *Cultural psychology* (pp. 569–606). Cambridge, UK: Cambridge University Press.

Gilligan, C. (1982). *In a different voice: Psychological theory and women's development.* Cambridge, MA: Harvard University Press.

Giroux, H. (1985). Marxism and schooling: The limits of radical educational discourse. *Education Theory, 34*(2), 113–135.

Giroux, H. (1988). Border pedagogy in the age of postmodernism. *Journal of Education, 20*(3), 162–181.

Giroux, H. (1991). *Postmodernism, feminist and cultural politics.* Albany, NY: SUNY Press.

Giroux, H. (1992). *Border crossings: Cultural workers and the politics of education.* New York: Routledge.

Giroux, H. (1994). Cultural studies. *Harvard Educational Review, 64*(3), 278–308.

Gore, J. (1993). *The struggle for pedagogies: Critical and feminist discourse as regimes of truth.* New York: Routledge.

Greene, M. (1988). *The dialectic of freedom.* New York: Teachers College Press.

Haraway, D. (1988). Situated knowledges: The science question in feminism and the privilege of partial perspective. *Feminist Studies, 14*(3), 575–599.

Haraway, D. (1989). *Primate visions: Gender, race and nature in the world of modern science.* New York: Routledge.

Harding, S. (1986). *The science question in feminism.* Ithaca, NY: Cornell University Press.

Harding, S. (1987). *Feminism and methodology.* Bloomington: Indiana University Press.

Harding, S. (1989). Is there a feminist method? In Nancy Tuana (Ed.), *Science and feminism* (pp. 17–32). Bloomington: Indiana University Press.

Harding, S. (1991). *Whose science? Whose knowledge? Thinking from women's lives.* Ithaca, NY: Cornell University Press.

Hartsock, N. (1990). Foucault on power: A theory for women? In L. J. Nicholson (Ed.), *Feminism/postmodernism* (pp. 157–175). New York: Routledge.

Hazelwood, C. (1996). *Shaping identities in school science: A narrative study of girls of Mexican origin.* Unpublished doctoral dissertation, Michigan State University.

Hollingsworth, S. (1994a). *Repositioning the teacher in US schools and society: Femi-*

nist readings of action research. Paper prepared for a keynote address at the Meeting of the Collaborative Action Research Network, University of Birmingham, UK.

Hollingsworth, S. (1994b). *Teacher research and urban literacy education*. New York: Teachers College Press.

hooks, b. (1981). *Ain't I a woman: Black women and feminisms*. Boston: South End Press.

hooks, b. (1990). *Yearning: Race, gender and cultural politics*. Boston: South End Press.

hooks, b. (1994). *Teaching to transgress: Education as a practice of freedom*. London: Routledge.

Howes, E. (1995). *To be a good scientist: High school students' ideas about the nature of science*. Paper presented at the Annual Meeting of the American Educational Research Association, San Francisco, CA.

Howes, E. (1997). *Prenatal testing in a feminist high school biology class*. Paper proposal for the Annual Meeting of the American Educational Research Association, Chicago, IL.

Hubbard, R. (1990). *The politics of women's biology*. New Brunswick and London: Rutgers University Press.

Hubbard, R. (1986, April/May). Facts and feminism—Thoughts on the masculinity of natural science. *Science for the People*, pp. 16–20.

Hurn, C. J. (1985). *The limits and possibilities of school* (2nd ed.). Boston: Allyn & Bacon.

Jacobs, M. (1994). *Revisiting lived experience: Postcard from the edge of the patriarchal wilderness*. Paper presented at the Journal of Curriculum Theory Conference, Banff, Alberta, Canada.

Jarvis, P. (1993). *Adult education and the state*. New York: Routledge.

Jarvis, P. (1995). *Adult and continuing education: Theory and practice*. New York: Routledge.

Kahle, J., & Meece, J. (1994). Research on girls in science lessons and applications. In D. Gabel (Ed.), *Handbook of research in science teaching and learning*. Washington, DC: National Science Teachers Association.

Kincheloe, J. (1993). *Toward a critical politics of teacher thinking: Mapping the postmodern*. Westport, CT: Bergin & Garvey.

Labaree, D. (1988). *The making of an American high school*. New York: Yale University Press.

Lather, P. (1988). Feminist perspectives on empowering research methodologies. *Women's Studies International Forum, 11*(6), 569–581.

Lather, P. (1991). *Getting Smart: Feminist research and pedagogy with/in the postmodern*. New York: Routledge.

Leistyna, P., & Woodrum, A. (1996). Context and culture: What is critical pedagogy? In P. Leistyna, A. Woodrum, & S. Sherblom (Eds.), *Breaking free: The transformative power of critical pedagogy* (pp. 1–12). Cambridge, MA: Harvard Education Review.

Lewis, M. (1993). *Without a word: Teaching beyond women's silence*. London: Routledge.

Lewis, M., & Simon, R. (1986). "A discourse not intended for her": Teaching and learning within patriarchy. *Harvard Educational Review, 56*(4), 26–29.

Longino, H. (1989). Can there be a feminist science? In Nancy Tuana (Ed.), *Science and feminism* (pp. 45–57). Bloomington: Indiana University Press.

Longino, H. (1990). *Science as social knowledge: values and objectivity in scientific inquiry.* Princeton, NJ: Princeton University Press.

Luke, C., & Gore, J. (1992). Introduction. In Luke and Gore (Eds.), *Feminisms and critical pedagogy* (pp. 1–14). New York: Routledge.

Luttrell, W. (1993). "The teachers, they all had their pets": Concepts of gender, knowledge and power. *Signs, 18*(3), 505–546.

Lytle, S., & Cochran-Smith, M. (1992). Teacher research as a way of knowing. *Harvard Educational Review, 62*(4), 447–474.

MacIntosh, P. (1980). *Feeling like a fraud.* Stone Center Occasional Paper. Wellesley, MA: Center for Research on Women.

Maher, F., & Tetreault, M. (1993). Doing feminist ethnography: Lessons from a feminist classroom. *Qualitative Studies in Education, 6*(1), 19–32.

Maher, F., & Tetreault, M. (1994). *Feminist classrooms.* New York: Basic Books.

Martin, J. (1988). Science in a different style. *American Philosophy Quarterly, 25*(2), 129–140.

Mercer, K. (1990). Back to my routes: A postscript to the 80s. *Ten-8, 2*(3), 32–39.

Merriam, S., & Cunningham, P. (1989). *Handbook of adult and continuing education.* San Francisco: Jossey-Bass.

Middleton, S. (1993). *Educating feminists: Life histories and pedagogy.* New York: Teachers College Press.

Miller, J. (1990). *Creating spaces and finding voices: Teachers collaborating for empowerment.* Albany, NY: SUNY Press.

Mohanty, C. T. (1994). On race and voice: Challenges for liberal education in the 1990s. In H. Giroux & P. McLaren (Eds.), *Between borders: Pedagogy and the politics of cultural studies* (pp. 145–166). New York: Routledge.

Mullis, I., & Jenkins, L. (1988). *The science report card: Elements of risk and recovery.* Report No. 17-S-01. Princeton, NJ: Educational Testing Service.

National Research Council [NRC]. (1996). *National Science Education Standards.* Washington, DC: National Academy Press.

Oakes, J. (1990). *Multiplying Inequalities: The effects of race, social class, and tracking on opportunities to learn mathematics and science.* Santa Monica, CA: Rand Corporation.

Oakes, J. (1985). *Keeping track.* New Haven: Yale University Press.

Orner, M. (1992). Interrupting calls for student voice in liberatory education: A feminist poststructural perspective. In C. Luke & J. Gore (Eds.), *Feminisms and critical pedagogy* (pp. 74–89). New York: Routledge.

Osborne, M. (1995). *The relevance of personal experience in science teaching? The teacher's responsibilities.* Paper presented at the annual meeting of the American Educational Research Association, San Francisco.

Osborne, M. (1997). Teaching and knowing: Dilemmas of constructivist science teaching. *Journal of Curriculum Studies, 29*(2), 183–196.

Osborne, M. (in press). *Constructing and framing knowledge in the elementary school classroom: Teachers, students and science.* New York: Peter Lang.

Patthey-Chavez, G. (1993). High school as an arena for cultural conflict and acculturation for Latino Angelinos. *Anthropology and Education Quarterly, 24*(1), 33–60.

Prelli, L. (1989). *A rhetoric of science: Inventing science discourse.* Columbia: University of South Carolina Press.

Rommetveit, R. (1980). On 'meanings' of acts and what is meant and made known by what is said in a pluralistic world. In M. Brenner (Ed.), *The structure of action.* New York: St. Martin's Press.

Roth, K. J. (1995). *Stories of alienation and connection: Examining the neighborhood of science from the margins.* Paper presented at the annual meeting of the American Educational Research Association, San Francisco.

Roychoudhury, A., Tippins, D., & Nichols, S. (1993). An Exploratory attempt toward a feminist pedagogy for science education. *Action in Teacher Education, 15*(4), 36–45.

Roychoudhury, A., Tippins, D., & Nichols, S. (1995). Gender-inclusive science teaching: A feminist constructive perspective. *Journal of Research in Science Teaching, 32*(9), 897–930.

Rubenson, K. (1989). Sociology of adult education. In S. Merriam & P. Cunningham (Eds.), *Handbook of adult and continuing education* (pp. 47–60). San Francisco: Jossey-Bass.

Rutherford, J. (1990). *Identity, community, culture, difference.* London: Lawrence and Wishart.

Smith, D. (1987). *The everyday world as problematic.* Boston: Northeastern University Press.

Spender, D., & Sarah, E. (1980). *Learning to lose: Sexism and education.* London: Women's Press.

Stanley, W., & Brickhouse, N. (1995). Multiculturalism, universalism and science education. *Science Education, 78*(4), 387–398.

Toulmin, S. (1990). *Cosmopolis: The hidden agenda of modernity.* New York: Free Press.

Ulrich, L. T. (1990). *A midwife's tale: The life of Martha Ballard, based on her diary 1785–1812.* New York: Vintage Books.

Usher, R., Bryant, I., & Johnston, R. (1997). *Adult education and the postmodern challenge: Learning beyond the limits.* New York: Routledge.

van Manen, M. (1988). *Tales of the field: On writing ethnography.* Chicago: University of Chicago Press.

Weiler, K. (1988). *Women teaching for change: Gender, class, and power.* South Hadley, MA: Bergen and Garvey.

Welch, S. (1985). *Communities of resistance and solidarity: A feminist theology of liberation.* New York: Orbis Books.

Willis, P. (1977). *Learning to Labor: How working-class kids get working-class jobs.* New York: Columbia University Press.

Women in Science Education [WISE]. (1994). *Revisioning boundaries in science education.* Symposium conducted at the meeting of the American Educational Research Association, New Orleans.

Women in Science Education. (1995). *Revisioning boundaries in science education from a feminist perspective: Continuing the conversation.* Symposium conducted at the meeting of the American Educational Research Association, San Francisco.

Women in Science Education. (1996). *Feminism and activism in science education.* Proposal for symposium at the National Association for Research in Science Teaching Conference, Chicago, IL.

Young, D., & Fraser, B. (1994). Gender differences in science achievement. *Journal for Research in Science Teaching, 31*(8), 857–871.

Index

About the Author

Angela Calabrese Barton is an assistant professor in the Program in Science Education at Teachers College, Columbia University. Her teaching and research interests involve understanding how intersections of race, class, and gender inform and challenge ideas and practices in science and science education. In addition to exploring these themes in school science, she is exploring these themes with children in urban settings and out-of-school contexts. She received her Ph.D. in Curriculum, Teaching and Education Policy from Michigan State University in East Lansing. Before that, she worked as a chemist in the biotechnology industry, as a chemistry teacher at the community college level, and as a teacher in after-school programs.